Mastering Ninject for Dependency Injection

Learn how Ninject facilitates the implementation
of Dependency Injection to solve common design
problems of real-life applications

Daniel Baharestani

BIRMINGHAM - MUMBAI

Mastering Ninject for Dependency Injection

First published: September 2013

Production Reference: 1190913

Published by Packt Publishing Ltd.
Livery Place
35 Livery Street
Birmingham B3 2PB, UK..

ISBN 978-1-78216-620-7

www.packtpub.com

Cover Image by Daniel Baharestani (baharestani@gmail.com) and Sheetal Aute (sheetala@packtpub.com)

Credits

Author

Daniel Baharestani

Reviewers

Remo Gloor

Daniel Allen

Matt Duffield

Ted Winslow

Acquisition Editor

Pramila Balan

Commissioning Editor

Nikhil Chinnari

Technical Editors

Iram Malik

Krishnaveni Haridas

Veena Pagare

Project Coordinator

Romal Karani

Proofreader

Clyde Jenkins

Indexer

Monica Ajmera

Graphics

Ronak Dhruv

Production Coordinator

Conidon Miranda

Cover Work

Conidon Miranda

About the Author

Daniel Baharestani is an experienced IT professional living in Australia. He has a BSc in software engineering and has over 10 years of professional experience in design and development of enterprise applications, mostly focused on Microsoft technologies. Daniel is currently working at 3P Learning, which is a global leader in online learning for school-aged students with its flagship platform, Mathletics—used by more than 3.5 million students in over 10,000 schools worldwide.

A book is like a song, which may usually be referred to by its singer's name, whereas many people are involved in the background to make it happen.

First, I am deeply indebted to my wife, Mona, who has taken all my responsibilities during this period. I understand how hard it was for her to do everything alone that we used to do together.

My special thanks goes to Remo Gloor, the main developers of Ninject, who kindly accepted the final technical review of this book, and other technical reviewers, including Daniel Allen, Matt Duffield, and Ted Winslow for providing valuable feedback.

I would also like to thank my manager, Houman, for being helpful and encouraging, and for understanding how important this book was to me. It would be much difficult to have it done without his support.

Finally, I should acknowledge the whole Packt team, who gave me this opportunity and guided me through this process, including but definitely not limited to, Nikhil Chinnari and Yogesh Dalvi, my commissioning editors, Sneha Modi and Romal Karani, my project coordinators, and Shrutika Kalbag, the author relationship executive for opening a door.

About the Reviewers

Remo Gloor has worked as a Software Architect at bbv Software Services AG in Switzerland for many years. During this time, he was using Ninject in several projects. At the beginning, he was a user of Ninject. Later, he contributed with several extensions. In 2010, he became manager and the main contributor to Ninject, which was developed originally by Nate Kohari and Ian Davis.

Besides his interest in dependency injection and IoC containers, he has also a strong interest in service-oriented and message-driven architectures, as well as event sourcing. Because of this, he contributed to the ActiveMq support to NServiceBus.

He blogs on `http://www.planetgeek.ch/author/remo-gloor/` mainly about Ninject. He also answers many Ninject-related questions on stackoverflow: `http://stackoverflow.com/users/448580/remo-gloor`.

Daniel Allen is a Chicago-based developer who specializes in ASP.NET MVC 4 development and enterprise architecture design. He develops primarily in C#, JavaScript, and Objective-C. Because of his heavy focus on enterprise architecture design, Dan has experience in an array of patterns and tools that he has effectively and logically combined together to meet a project's unique needs. Dan holds a B.S. in Management Information Systems and an MBA with a concentration in Information Systems.

Dan spends much of his free time working on development-related side contracts and searching for the next great startup idea. He aspires to start a consulting firm that will provide capital for the various startup ideas one day. For recreation, he enjoys training and competing in various marathons, and aspires to complete a full iron man competition one day.

He has formerly worked with Millennium Information Services, Inc. as an ASP. NET MVC Web Developer. His primary tasks in this role were MVC 4 Razor development, HTML 5 frontend GUI design, enterprise architecture design, and WCF, Oracle database, and agile development. He has also worked for Arc Worldwide / Leo Burnett as an Associate Software Engineer. His primary tasks in this role were ASP.NET Web Forms development, frontend GUI design, and he also worked on SQL Server database. Dan has also worked with American Concrete Pavement Association as a Software Engineer. His primary tasks in this role were ASP.NET Web Forms and MVC 4 development, iOS mobile development, and SQL Server database, graphics and media development.

For Dan's complete professional history and his online interactive portfolio, please visit `http://www.apexwebz.com`.

I would like to thank my family for their ongoing support. My father inspired me to start working in this field, and now I can't picture myself doing anything else. I would also like to thank my close friend, past boss, and ongoing mentor, Robert Rodden, for helping me at every step of the way in my professional career.

Matt Duffield is a software architect, and has over 17 years of experience working in IT. He enjoys building a rich line of business applications that focus on great user experiences while providing excellent business intelligence, such as dashboards and expert systems. His current focus is on client-side MVC architecture and building cross-platform solutions. Matt is very active in the community, speaking at user groups and code camps. He is an INETA speaker and a Microsoft MVP in client development. He is the co-author of *Microsoft Silverlight 5: Building Rich Enterprise Dashboards, Packt Publishing*. His blog can be found at `http://mattduffield.wordpress.com`. You can follow him on Twitter at `@mattduffield`. Matt is also the leader of the Charlotte ALT.NET user group (`http://www.meetup.com/charlottealtnet/`) and Charlotte Game Dev user group (`http://www.meetup.com/Charlotte-Game-Dev/`). He is also the Vice President of the Charlotte Enterprise Developers Guild (`http://www.developersguild.org/`) and also board member of the Carolina Code Camp.

Ted Winslow has been one of those programmers who impressed the likes of NASA and Boeing with his skills behind a keyboard ever since his sixth grade. Even when he isn't working for one of the big names, he's freelancing for multimillion-dollar shops, and considers writing code a way to relax in his downtime. He started writing code while young and did it with little more than a basic starter book and a half-broken computer. Against all odds, he has now a lengthy and respected work history with code chops for which large and small companies hunger. Nowadays, he's spotted helping people in his free time to make sure the young programmers understand and have a chance to live their dream, even when the odds are stacked against them.

> I'd like to thank my friends for both the encouragement they've provided during my career and for putting up with me every day. You all mean a lot to me.

www.PacktPub.com

Support files, eBooks, discount offers and more

You might want to visit www.PacktPub.com for support files and downloads related to your book.

Did you know that Packt offers eBook versions of every book published, with PDF and ePub files available? You can upgrade to the eBook version at www.PacktPub.com and as a print book customer, you are entitled to a discount on the eBook copy. Get in touch with us at service@ packtpub.com for more details.

At www.PacktPub.com, you can also read a collection of free technical articles, sign up for a range of free newsletters and receive exclusive discounts and offers on Packt books and eBooks.

http://PacktLib.PacktPub.com

Do you need instant solutions to your IT questions? PacktLib is Packt's online digital book library. Here, you can access, read and search across Packt's entire library of books.

Why Subscribe?

- Fully searchable across every book published by Packt
- Copy and paste, print and bookmark content
- On demand and accessible via web browser

Free Access for Packt account holders

If you have an account with Packt at www.PacktPub.com, you can use this to access PacktLib today and view nine entirely free books. Simply use your login credentials for immediate access.

Table of Contents

Preface   **1**

Chapter 1: Understanding Dependency Injection   **7**

  What is Dependency Injection?   **8**

    DI or Inversion of Control (IoC)   9

  How can DI help?   **10**

  My First DI Application   **12**

  DI Containers   **16**

  Why use Ninject?   **17**

  Summary   **17**

Chapter 2: Getting Started with Ninject   **19**

  Hello Ninject!   **19**

  It's all about Binding   **22**

  Object Lifetime   **25**

    Transient scope   25

    Singleton scope   26

    Thread scope   27

    Request scope   28

    Custom scope   28

  Ninject modules   **30**

  XML configuration   **31**

    How to use XML configuration   31

  Convention over configuration   **34**

    Selecting the assemblies   35

    Selecting the components   36

      Filtering the selected components   37

      Explicit inclusion and exclusion   37

    Selecting service types   37

    Configuring the Bindings   38

  Summary   **39**

Chapter 3: Meeting Real-world Requirements   41

DI patterns and antipatterns   41
Constructor Injection   42
Initializer methods and properties   43
Service Locator   45
Multi binding and contextual binding   46
Implementing the plugin model   46
Contextual binding   49
    Named binding   51
    Resolving metadata   52
    Attribute-based binding   55
    Target-based conditions   56
    Generic helper   57
Custom providers   57
Activation context   61
The Factory Method   61
Dynamic factories   62
The Shape Factory example   62
Using convention   65
    Selecting service types   65
    Defining Binding Generator   65
Telecom Switch example   66
Custom Instance Providers   68
Func   70
Lazy   71
Summary   71

Chapter 4: Ninject in Action   73

Windows Forms applications   77
WPF and Silverlight applications   81
ASP.NET MVC applications   89
Validator injection   92
Filter injection   94
    Conditional filtering (When)   97
    Contextual arguments (With)   98
WCF applications   98
ASP.NET Web Forms applications   102
Summary   103

Chapter 5: Doing More with Extensions   **105**

Interception   **105**
Setup Interception   106
Member Interception   106
Type Interception   108
Multiple Interceptors   110
InterceptAttribute   113
Mocking Kernel   **114**
Extending Ninject   **118**
Summary   **119**
Index   **121**

Preface

Mastering Ninject for Dependency Injection demonstrates how Ninject facilitates the implementation of Dependency Injection to solve common design problems of real-life applications in a simple and easy-to-understand format. This book will teach you everything you need in order to implement Dependency Injection using Ninject in a real-life project. Not only does it teach the Ninject core framework features which are essential for implementing DI, but it also explores the power of Ninject's most useful extensions, and demonstrates how to apply them in a real-life application.

What this book covers

Chapter 1, *Understanding Dependency Injection*, introduces Dependency Injection concepts and describes the advantages of using this technique. We will also go through a simple example and implement the principles and patterns related to DI techniques. After understanding what a DI container is, we will discuss why Ninject is a suitable choice.

Chapter 2, *Getting Started with Ninject*, teaches the user how to add Ninject to a practical project and how to use the basic features of this framework. The chapter starts with an example demonstrating how to set up and use Ninject in a Hello World project. Then, we will talk about how Ninject resolves dependencies and how it manages object lifetime. We will also cover the code-based configuration using Ninject modules and XML-based configuration. The final section of this chapter describes how to configure a large application which includes hundreds of services using Ninject conventions. By the end of this chapter, the user will be able to set up and use the basic features of Ninject.

Chapter 3, *Meeting Real-world Requirements*, introduces more advanced features of Ninject which are necessary in order to implement DI in real-world situations. The chapter starts with an introduction to some patterns and antipatterns related to Ninject. We will then go through real examples and see how Ninject can solve such kind of problems. By the end of this chapter, the user is expected to know almost all of the significant features of Ninject.

Chapter 4, *Ninject in Action*, shows how to set up different types of applications using Ninject. We will implement a concrete scenario using a variety of application types, including but not limited to, WPF, ASP .NET MVC, and WCF, to see how to set up and use Ninject for injecting the dependencies. By the end of this chapter, the user should be able to set up and use Ninject for all kinds of described applications.

Chapter 5, *Doing More with Extensions*, will show how Interception is a solution for cross-cutting concerns, and how to use Mocking Kernel as a test asset. While the core library of Ninject is kept clean and simple, Ninject is a highly extensible DI container, and it is possible to extend its power by using extension plugins. We will also see how Ninject can be extended.

What you need for this book

The examples of the book are written in Microsoft Visual Studio 2012; however, the target framework is set to .NET 4.0 so that they can be easily built using MSBuild and .NET Framework 4.0, even if you do not have Visual Studio 2012.

In the ASP.NET MVC application, we used MVC 3, and Microsoft SQL Server Compact 4.0 is used for SQL Data Layer.

You need an Internet connection to download required references and online packages, such as Ninject and its extensions. Having NuGet package manager on your system facilitates installing of referenced packages, but it is not required, as wherever we need to install such packages, the instruction for manually downloading and referencing the binaries is also provided.

We have also used NUnit for our Unit Tests, which is freely available for download via NuGet or NUnit website.

Who this book is for

This book is for all software developers and architects who are willing to create maintainable, loosely coupled, extensible, and testable applications. Because Ninject targets the .NET platform, this book is not suitable for software developers of other platforms. You should be comfortable with object oriented principals, and have a fair understanding of inheritance and abstraction. Being familiar with design patterns and general concept of unit testing is also a great help, but no knowledge of Dependency Injection is assumed. Although Ninject can be used in any .NET programming languages, the examples of this book are all in C#, so the reader is assumed to be familiar with this language.

Conventions

In this book, you will find a number of styles of text that distinguish between different kinds of information. Here are some examples of these styles, and an explanation of their meaning.

Code words in text are shown as follows: "The following example shows how to use the ILogger interface."

A block of code is set as follows:

```
[Inject]
public ILogger Logger {get; set;}

public void DoSomething()
{
    Logger.Debug("Doing something...");
}
```

When we wish to draw your attention to a particular part of a code block, the relevant lines or items are set in bold:

```
kernel.Bind(x => x
    .FromThisAssembly()
    .SelectAllClasses()
    .InNamespaces("Northwind.Controllers")
    .BindBase());
```

Any command-line input or output is written as follows:

```
2013-05-23 05:04:40 INFO  LogSamples.Consumer - Doing something...
```

New terms and **important words** are shown in bold. Words that you see on the screen, in menus or dialog boxes for example, appear in the text like this: "The first one is called when the hyperlink **Create New** is clicked using HTTP GET method ".

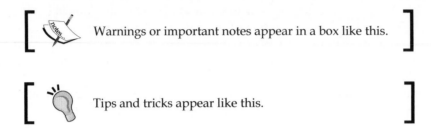

Warnings or important notes appear in a box like this.

Tips and tricks appear like this.

Reader feedback

Feedback from our readers is always welcome. Let us know what you think about this book—what you liked or may have disliked. Reader feedback is important for us to develop titles that you really get the most out of.

To send us general feedback, simply send an e-mail to feedback@packtpub.com, and mention the book title through the subject of your message.

If there is a topic that you have expertise in and you are interested in either writing or contributing to a book, see our author guide on www.packtpub.com/authors.

Customer support

Now that you are the proud owner of a Packt book, we have a number of things to help you to get the most from your purchase.

Downloading the example code

You can download the example code files for all Packt books you have purchased from your account at http://www.packtpub.com. If you purchased this book elsewhere, you can visit http://www.packtpub.com/support and register to have the files e-mailed directly to you.

Errata

Although we have taken every care to ensure the accuracy of our content, mistakes do happen. If you find a mistake in one of our books—maybe a mistake in the text or the code—we would be grateful if you would report this to us. By doing so, you can save other readers from frustration and help us improve subsequent versions of this book. If you find any errata, please report them by visiting http://www.packtpub.com/support, selecting your book, clicking on the **errata submission form** link, and entering the details of your errata. Once your errata are verified, your submission will be accepted and the errata will be uploaded to our website, or added to any list of existing errata, under the Errata section of that title.

Piracy

Piracy of copyright material on the Internet is an ongoing problem across all media. At Packt, we take the protection of our copyright and licenses very seriously. If you come across any illegal copies of our works, in any form, on the Internet, please provide us with the location address or website name immediately so that we can pursue a remedy.

Please contact us at copyright@packtpub.com with a link to the suspected pirated material.

We appreciate your help in protecting our authors, and our ability to bring you valuable content.

Questions

You can contact us at questions@packtpub.com if you are having a problem with any aspect of the book, and we will do our best to address it.

1

Understanding
Dependency Injection

"It's more about a way of thinking and designing code than it is about tools and techniques"

– Mark Seemann

This chapter introduces the **Dependency Injection (DI)** concepts and describes the advantages of using this pattern. We will also go through a simple example and implement the principles and patterns related to the DI technique to it. After understanding what a DI container is, we will discuss why Ninject is a suitable one.

By the end of this chapter, the reader is expected to have a good understanding of DI and how Ninject can help them as a DI container.

The topics covered in this chapter are:

- What is Dependency Injection?
- How can DI help?
- My first DI application
- DI Containers
- Why use Ninject?

What is Dependency Injection?

Dependency Injection is one of the techniques in software engineering which improves the maintainability of a software application by managing the dependent components. In order to have a better understanding of this pattern, let's start this section with an example to clarify what is meant by a dependency, and what other elements are involved in this process.

Cameron is a skilled carpenter who spends most of his time creating wooden stuffs. Today, he is going to make a chair. He needs a saw, a hammer, and other tools. During the process of creating the chair, he needs to figure out what tool he needs and find it in his toolbox. Although what he needs to focus on is how to make a chair, without thinking of what tools he needs and how to find them, it is not possible to finish the construction of the chair.

The following code is the C# representation of Cameron, as a carpenter:

```csharp
class Carpenter
{
  Saw saw = new Saw();
  void MakeChair()
  {
    saw.Cut();
    // ...
  }
}
```

Sarah is a heart surgeon. She works for a hospital and spends her days in the operation room, and today she is going to perform an open-heart surgery. It is a sophisticated procedure, and she needs to focus on the operation itself, rather than finding the tools during the operation. That is why she has an assistant to provide her with the tools she requires. This way, she ensures that the exact tool that she needs will be in her hand by her assistant. She doesn't need to know where the tool is and how to find it. These are her assistant's responsibilities.

Downloading the example code

You can download the example code files for all Packt books you have purchased from your account at http://www.packtpub.com. If you purchased this book elsewhere, you can visit http://www.packtpub.com/support and register to have the files e-mailed directly to you.

This is the C# implementation of Sarah, the surgeon:

```csharp
class Surgeon
{
  private Forceps forceps;

  // The forceps object will be injected into the constructor
  // method by a third party while the class is being created.
  public Surgeon(Forceps forceps)
  {
    this.forceps = forceps;
  }

  public void Operate()
  {
    forceps.Grab();
    //...
  }
}
```

As we can see, she doesn't need to worry about how to get the forceps; they are provided to her by someone else.

In the previous examples, Cameron and Sarah are samples of dependent components that have a responsibility, and tools that they need are their dependencies. Dependency Injection is all about how they get to the tools they need. In the first example, the dependent component (Cameron) itself had to locate the dependency, while in the second one, a third party (the assistant) locates and provides it. This third party is called an Injector, which injects the dependencies.

DI or Inversion of Control (IoC)

Martin Fowler defines **Inversion of Control (IoC)** as a style of programming in which the framework takes the control of the flow instead of your code. Comparing handling an event to calling a function is a good example to understand IoC. When you call the functions of a framework, you are controlling the flow, because you decide in what sequence to call the functions. But in case of handling events, you are defining the functions and the framework is calling them, so the control is inverted to the framework instead of you. This example showed you how control can be inverted. DI is a specific type of IoC, because instead of your components concern about their dependencies, they are provided with the dependencies by the framework. Indeed, as Mark Seemann states in his book, *Dependency Injection in .NET*, IoC is a broader term which includes, but is not limited to, DI, even though they are often being used interchangeably. IoC is also known as the Hollywood Principle: "Don't call us, we'll call you".

How can DI help?

Every software application is inevitable of change. As your code grows and new requirements arrive, the importance of maintaining your codes becomes more tangible, and it is not possible for a software application to go on if it is not maintainable. One of the design principles that lead to producing a maintainable code is known as **Separation of Concerns (SoC)**. The SoC is a broad concept and is not limited to software design; but in the case of composing software components, we can think of SoC as implementing distinct classes, each of which deals with a single responsibility. In the first example, finding a tool is a different concern from doing the operation itself and separating these two concerns is one of the prerequisites for creating a maintainable code.

Separation of concerns, however, doesn't lead to a maintainable code if the sections that deal with concerns are tightly coupled to each other.

Although there are different types of forceps that Sarah may need during the operation, she doesn't need to mention the exact type of forceps which she requires. She just states that she needs forceps, and it is on her assistant to determine which forceps satisfies her need the best. If the exact type that Sarah needs is temporarily not available, the assistant has the freedom to provide her with another suitable type. If the hospital has bought a new type of forceps that the assistant thinks is more suitable, he or she can easily switch to the new one because he or she knows that Sarah doesn't care about the type of forceps as long as it is suitable. In other words, Sarah is not tightly coupled to a specific type of forceps.

The key principle leading to loose coupling is the following, from the Gang of Four (Erich Gamma, Richard Helm, Ralph Johnson, and John Vlissides, *Design Patterns: Elements of Reusable Object-Oriented Software*):

"Program to an "interface", not an "implementation"."

When we address our dependencies as abstract elements (an interface or abstract class), rather than concrete classes, we will be able to easily replace the concrete classes without affecting the consumer component:

```
class Surgeon
{
  private IForceps forceps;

  public Surgeon(IForceps forceps)
  {
    this.forceps = forceps;
  }
```

```
public void Operate()
{
  forceps.Grab();
  //...
}
}
```

The Surgeon class is addressing the interface IForceps and does not care about the exact type of the object injected into its constructer. The C# compiler ensures that the argument passed to the forceps parameter always implements the IForceps interface and therefore, existence of the Grab() method is guaranteed. The following code shows how an instance of Surgeon can be created providing with a suitable forceps:

```
var forceps = assistant.Get<IForceps>();
var surgeon = new Surgeon (forceps);
```

Because the Surgeon class is programmed to the IForceps interface rather than a certain type of forceps implementation, we can freely instantiate it with any type of forceps that the assistant object decides to provide.

As the previous example shows, loose coupling (surgeon is not dependent on a certain type of forceps) is a result of programming to interface (surgeon depends on IForceps) and separation of concerns, (choosing forceps is the assistant's concern, while the surgeon has other concerns) which increases the code maintainability.

Now that we know loose coupling increases the flexibility and gives freedom of replacing the dependencies easily; let's see what else we get out of this freedom other than maintainability. One of the advantages of being able to replace the concrete classes is testability. As long as the components are loosely coupled to their dependencies, we can replace the actual dependencies with **Test Doubles** such as mock objects. Test Doubles are simplified version of the real objects that look and behave like them and facilitate testing. The following example shows how to unit test the Surgeon class using a mock forceps as a Test Double:

```
[Test]
public void CallingOperateCallsGrabOnForceps()
{
  var forcepsMock = new Mock<IForceps>();

  var surgeon = new Surgeon(forcepsMock.Object);
  surgeon.Operate();

  forcepsMock.Verify(f => f.Grab());
}
```

In this unit test, an instance of the Surgeon class is being created as a **System Under Test (SUT)**, and the mock object is injected into its constructor. After calling the Operate method on the surgeon object, we ask our mock framework to verify whether the Grab operation is called on the mock forceps object as expected.

Maintainability and testability are two advantages of loose coupling, which is in turn a product of Dependency Injection. On the other hand, the way an Injector creates the instances of concrete types, can introduce the third benefit of DI, which is the late binding. An Injector is given a type and is expected to return an object instance of that type. It often uses reflection in order to activate objects. So, the decision of which type to activate can be delayed to the runtime. Late binding gives us the flexibility of replacing the dependencies without recompiling the application. Another benefit of DI is extensibility. Because classes depend on abstractions, we can easily extend their functionality by substituting the concrete dependencies.

My First DI Application

We start our example with a service class in which the concerns are not separated. Then we will improve maintainability step-by-step, by first separating concerns and then programming to interface in order to make our modules loosely coupled. At the final point, we will have our first DI application. The source code for all the examples of this book is available for download on the publisher's website.

The main responsibility of this service is to send an e-mail using the information provided. In order to make the example simple and clear, client initialization is omitted.

```
class MailService
{
  public void SendEmail(string address, string subject, string
    body)
  {
    var mail = new MailMessage();
    mail.To.Add(address);
    mail.Subject = subject;
    mail.Body = body;
    var client = new SmtpClient();
    // Setup client with smtp server address and port here
    client.Send(mail);
  }
}
```

Then, we add some logging to it, so that we know what is going on in our service:

```
class MailService
{
  public void SendMail(string address, string subject, string
    body)
  {
    Console.WriteLine("Creating mail message...");
    var mail = new MailMessage();
    mail.To.Add(address);
    mail.Subject = subject;
    mail.Body = body;
    var client = new SmtpClient();
    // Setup client with smtp server address and port here
    Console.WriteLine("Sending message...");
    client.Send(mail);
    Console.WriteLine("Message sent successfully.");
  }
}
```

After a little while, we find it useful to add time to our logs. In this example, sending the mail message and logging functionality are two different concerns which are addressed in a single class, and it is not possible to change the logging mechanism without touching the MailService class. Therefore, in order to add time to our logs, we have to change the MailService class. So, let's re-factor this class and separate the concern of logging from sending a mail prior to adding the time functionality:

```
class MailService
{
  private ConsoleLogger logger;
  public MailService()
  {
    logger = new ConsoleLogger();
  }

  public void SendMail(string address, string subject, string
    body)
  {
    logger.Log("Creating mail message...");
    var mail = new MailMessage();
    mail.To.Add(address);
    mail.Subject = subject;
    mail.Body = body;
    var client = new SmtpClient();
    // Setup client with smtp server address and port here
    logger.Log("Sending message...");
    client.Send(mail);
    logger.Log("Message sent successfully.");
  }
}
```

The ConsoleLogger class is only responsible for the logging mechanism, and this concern is removed from MailService. Now, it is possible to modify the logging mechanism without affecting MailService:

```
class ConsoleLogger
{
  public void Log(string message)
  {
    Console.WriteLine("{0}: {1}", DateTime.Now, message);
  }
}
```

Now, we need to write our logs in Windows Event Log rather than showing them in console. Looks like we need an EventLogger class as well:

```
class EventLogger
{
  public void Log(string message)
  {
    EventLog.WriteEntry("MailService", message);
  }
}
```

Although the concern of sending mail and logging are now separated in two different classes, MailService is still tightly coupled to the ConsoleLogger class, and it is not possible to replace its logger without modifying it. We are just one step away from breaking the tight coupling between the MailService and Logger classes. We should now introduce the dependencies as interfaces rather than concrete classes:

```
interface ILogger
{
  void Log(string message);
}
```

Both the ConsoleLogger and EventLogger classes should implement this interface:

```
class ConsoleLogger:ILogger
{
  public void Log(string message)
  {
    Console.WriteLine("{0}: {1}", DateTime.Now, message);
  }
}
class EventLogger:ILogger
{
```

```
    public void Log(string message)
    {
        EventLog.WriteEntry("MailService", message);
    }
}
```

Now, it is time to remove the references to the concrete `ConsoleLogger` class and address `ILogger` instead:

```
private ILogger logger;
public MailService()
{
    logger = new ILogger();
}
```

But the previous code won't compile because it doesn't make sense to instantiate an interface. We should introduce this dependency as a constructor parameter and have the concrete object injected into it by a third party:

```
public MailService(ILogger logger)
{
    this.logger = logger;
}
```

At this point, our classes are loosely coupled and we can change the loggers freely without affecting the `MailService` class. Using DI, we have also separated the concern of creating a new instance of the logger class, which includes the concern of deciding what concrete logger to use from the main responsibility of `MailService`, which is sending an e-mail:

```
internal class Program
{
    private static void Main(string[] args)
    {
        var mailService = new MailService(new EventLogger());
        mailService.SendMail("someone@somewhere.com", "My first DI
            App", "Hello World!");
    }
}
```

The main method of this application is where we decide what concrete objects to inject in our dependent classes. This (preferably) unique location in the application where modules are composed together is named `Composition Root` by Mark Seemann. For more information on DI, *Dependency Injection in .NET*, by *Mark Seemann* is recommended.

DI Containers

A DI container is an injector object that injects the dependencies into a dependent object. As we have seen in the previous example, we don't necessarily need a DI container in order to implement Dependency Injection. However, in more complex scenarios, a DI container can save a lot of time and effort by automating most of the tasks that we had to do manually. In real world applications, a single dependant class can have many dependencies, each of which have their own dependencies that forms a large graph of dependencies. A DI container should resolve the dependencies, and this is where the decision of selecting a concrete class for the given abstraction should be made. This decision is made by a mapping table, which is either based on a configuration file or is programmatically defined by the developer. We can see an example for both here:

```
<bind service="ILogger" to="ConsoleLogger" />
```

This one is an example of code-based configuration:

```
Bind<ILogger>().To<ConsoleLogger>();
```

We can also define conditional rules instead of just mapping a service to a concrete type. We will discuss this feature in detail in *Chapter 2, Getting Started with Ninject*.

A container has the responsibility of dealing with the lifetime of the created objects. It should know how long an object should be kept alive, when to dispose of it, in what condition to return the existing instance, and in what condition to create a new one.

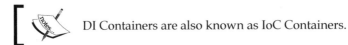 DI Containers are also known as IoC Containers.

There are other DI Container besides Ninject. You can find a list of them in Scott Hanselman's blog (`http://www.hanselman.com/blog/ListOfNETDependencyInjectionContainersIOC.aspx`). Unity, Castle Windsor, StructureMap, Spring.NET, and Autofac are a few of them:

	Unity	Castle Windsor	StructureMap	Spring.NET	Autofac
License	MS-PL	Apache 2	Apache 2	Apache 2	MIT
Description	Build on the "kernel" of ObjectBuilder.	Well documented and used by many.	Written by Jeremy D. Miller.	Written by Mark Pollack.	Written by Nicholas Blumhardt and Rinat Abdullin.

Why use Ninject?

Ninject is a lightweight Dependency Injection framework for .NET applications. It helps you split your application into a collection of loosely-coupled, highly-cohesive pieces, and then glues them back together in a flexible manner. By using Ninject to support your software's architecture, your code will become easier to write, reuse, test, and modify. Instead of relying on reflection for invocation, Ninject takes advantage of lightweight code generation in the **CLR** (**Common Language Runtime**). This can result in a dramatic (8-50x) improvement in performance in many situations. Ninject includes many advanced features. For example, Ninject was the first dependency injector to support contextual binding, in which a different concrete implementation of a service may be injected, depending on the context in which it is requested. Ninject supports most major facilities offered by the competing frameworks (although, many such elements live in *extensions:* plugin modules that layer on facilities on top of the core). You can have a look at the Ninject official wiki at `https://github.com/ninject/ninject/wiki` for a more detailed list of Ninject features which makes it one of the top DI containers.

Summary

Dependency Injection is a technique to help us produce loosely coupled code by moving the concern of creating the dependencies to another object known as a DI container. In other words, instead of a dependent object to decide what concrete class it needs, it just states the needs as an abstraction, and the injector provides it with the most suitable concrete class that satisfies the needs. Loose coupling is one of the main advantages of DI that leads to extensibility, maintainability, and testability. Late binding is another benefit of DI and dynamic loading of plugins is an example of this feature. There are DI containers other than Ninject, each of which has their own advantages and disadvantages.

2

Getting Started with Ninject

This chapter teaches the user how to add Ninject to a practical project and use the basic features of this framework. The chapter starts with an example demonstrating how to setup and use Ninject in a Hello World project. Then, we will talk about how Ninject resolves dependencies and how it manages object lifetime. Final sections of this chapter will cover code-based configuration using Ninject modules and XML-based configuration using an XML file. By the end of this chapter, the user will be able to setup and use basic features of Ninject.

The topics covered in this chapter are:

- Hello Ninject!
- It's all about Binding
- Object Lifetime
- Ninject modules
- XML configuration
- Convention over configuration

Hello Ninject!

Although DI is for complex projects, and applying it to a simple project looks like over-engineering, a Hello World project should usually be as simple as possible to show only how a framework works. This project helps us understand how to setup Ninject and run it in the simplest way. So, if you have already used Ninject and are familiar with this process, you can skip this section and continue reading the next one.

1. The first step to setup Ninject is to download Ninject library. You can do it either using NuGet or by downloading the binary file. If you have NuGet package manager, create a new Console Application project in Visual Studio, and then simply search for Ninject in NuGet UI to install the package, as the following figure illustrates. Alternatively, you can type `install-package Ninject,` and then press enter in the Packet Manager Console located at **View | Other Windows** menu. Once the installation of Ninject package is finished, jump to step 5. If you don't have NuGet package manager, go to the download page of Ninject official website (`http://www.ninject.org/download.html`) and download the most recent version for your desired framework. Considering Ninject is an open source project, you can even download the source codes from GitHub via the link provided on the download page.

2. In Windows Vista and other newer versions of Windows, you need to unblock the downloaded archive prior to uncompressing it, in order to prevent further security issues at runtime. Simply right-click on the downloaded file, open **Properties**, and from the **General** tab, click on the **Unblock** button. Then, unzip the archive to your libraries directory (for example, `D:\Libraries\Ninject`).

3. Open Visual Studio and create a new Console Application project.

4. Add a reference to `Ninject.dll` in your library directory.

5. Add a new class to your project and call it `SalutationService`:

```
class SalutationService
{
  public void SayHello()
  {
    Console.WriteLine("Hello Ninject!");
  }
}
```

6. Add using Ninject to the using section of `Program.cs`.

7. Add the following lines to your `Main` method:

```
using (var kernel = new Ninject.StandardKernel())
{
  var service = kernel.Get<SalutationService>();
  service.SayHello();
}
```

8. Run the application.

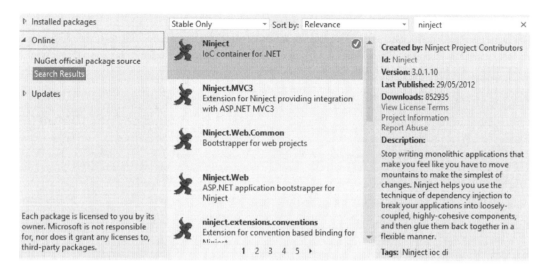

That is how Ninject works in the simplest way. We didn't even need to add any configuration or annotation. Although we didn't have anything to inject in the previous example, Ninject did its main job, which was resolving a type (SalutationService).

Let's have a look at the Main method to see what was happening there. In the first line, we created a kernel object by instantiating StandardKernel. Kernel is always the start point of creating our dependency graph. In this simple example, the graph only consists of one type, which is SalutationService. As we see, we didn't call the constructor of SalutationService in neither of the Main method lines. Instead, we asked our container (kernel) to do it for us. We gave our required type to the Get method, and it returned an instance of the given type. In other words, the Get method was provided with the root type (SalutationService) of our dependency graph and returned the graph object.

Now that we know how to setup Ninject, let's move ahead to a more complex example to see how Ninject helps us to implement DI better.

It's all about Binding

In *Chapter 1, Understanding Dependency Injection*, we implemented DI manually in the `MailService` class. You remember that we ignored the configuration of `SmtpClient` to simplify the project. Now, we are going to add the configuration of `SmtpClient` and implement DI using Ninject.

Let's start by creating the `MailConfig` class:

```
class MailServerConfig
{
  public string SmtpServer
  {
    get
    {
      return ConfigurationManager.AppSettings["SmtpServer"];
    }
  }

  public int SmtpPort
  {
    get
    {
      var port = ConfigurationManager
      .AppSettings["SmtpPort"];
      return Convert.ToInt32(port);
    }
  }

  public string SenderEmail
  {
    get
    {
      return ConfigurationManager
      .AppSettings["SenderEmail"];
    }
  }

  public string SenderPassword
  {
    get
    {
      return ConfigurationManager
      .AppSettings["SenderPassword"];
    }
  }
}
```

Now, we can update the `MailService` class and incorporate `MailServiceConfig`:

```
class MailService
{
  private ILogger logger;
  private SmtpClient client;
  private string sender;

  public MailService(MailServerConfig config, ILogger logger)
  {
    this.logger = logger;
    InitializeClient(config);
    sender = config.SenderEmail;
  }

  public void SendMail(string address, string subject, string
    body)
  {
    logger.Log("Initializing...");
    var mail = new MailMessage(sender, address);
    mail.Subject = subject;
    mail.Body = body;
    logger.Log("Sending message...");
    client.Send(mail);
    logger.Log("Message sent successfully.");
  }

  private void InitializeClient(MailServerConfig config)
  {
    client = new SmtpClient();
    client.Host = config.SmtpServer;
    client.Port = config.SmtpPort;
    client.EnableSsl = true;
    var credentials = new NetworkCredential();
    credentials.UserName = config.SenderEmail;
    credentials.Password = config.SenderPassword;
    client.Credentials = credentials;
  }
}
```

The class consists of two methods and one constructor. The `SendMail` method is not changed so much, except that it is no more instantiating `SmtpClient` and is using the new introduced client field.

We have added a new method called `InitializeClient`, which instantiates and initializes the client field using the given `MailServerConfig` object.

The constructor has been added another parameter, which accepts an object of `MailServerConfig`, which contains some settings obtained from the application configuration file.

The following figure shows the dependency graph of this application:

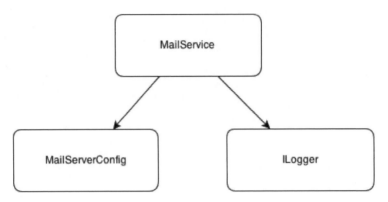

Now, let's see how Ninject is going to resolve the dependencies and create the graph object. Considering the last example, we need a kernel object and give it the starting node of our graph, so that it returns the entire graph as the following code shows:

```
var kernel = new StandardKernel();
var mailService = kernel.Get<MailService>();
```

Ninject starts by resolving the `MailService` type. It finds the type and realizes that in order to instantiate it, first it should create an instance of `MailServerConfig` and `ILogger`. That is because Ninject automatically creates arguments that should be passed to the constructor of the type being instantiated. It injects these arguments to the constructor parameters without us having to instruct it to do so. Creating an instance of `MailServerConfig` is as easy as calling its only constructor, but what about `ILogger`? `ILogger` is an interface, and it is not possible to create an instance of an interface itself. Also, it may have multiple implementations. So, how is Ninject supposed to know which implementation of `ILogger` to use?

Ninject uses its Binding system to decide what implementation to use for a given type. A binding is an instruction which maps one type (usually an abstract type or an interface) to a concrete type that matches such a given type. This process is also called **Service Registration**.

The following code instructs Ninject how to resolve `ILogger`:

```
kernel.Bind<ILogger>().To<ConsoleLogger>();
```

It means that Ninject should always use the `ConsoleLogger` type as an implementation type for the `ILogger` type.

The final `Main` method's body looks like this:

```
using (var kernel = new StandardKernel())
{
  kernel.Bind<ILogger>().To<ConsoleLogger>();
  var mailService = kernel.Get<MailService>();
  mailService.SendMail("someone@domain.com", "Hi", null);
}
```

 If multiple services should be bound to a single component, use this syntax:

```
kernel.Bind<IService1,IService2>().To<MyService>();
```

Object Lifetime

One of the responsibilities of a DI container is to manage the lifetime of objects that it creates. It should decide when to create a new instance of the given type and when to use an existing instance. It should also take care of disposing of objects when they are not used anymore. Ninject has a strong support for managing Object Lifetime in different situations. Whenever we define a binding, we can declare the scope of the object instance being created. Within that scope, the object instance will be reused and exist exactly once for each binding. Note that an object is not allowed to have a dependency on an object with shorter lifetime.

Transient scope

In Transient scope, the object lifetime is not managed by Ninject. Whenever we request an instance of a type, a new one will be created. Ninject doesn't take care of keeping the created instance or disposing of it in this scope. This is the default object scope in Ninject. If no scope is explicitly specified, they are transient-scoped. In the previous code, both `ConsoleLogger` and `MailService` were treated in the Transient scope because the object scope was not specified.

Singleton scope

In the previous example, the ILogger interface is bound to the ConsoleLogger class, which means whenever Ninject encounters ILogger, it should create a new instance of ConsoleLogger. But we don't really need multiple instances of ConsoleLogger in all of the classes that need to log to console. Looks like it is a good idea to make ConsoleLogger singleton. There are two approaches to achieve this. The first one is using one of the *Singleton* patterns:

```
class ConsoleLogger:ILogger
{
  public static readonly ConsoleLogger Instance = new ConsoleLogger();

  private static ConsoleLogger()
  {
    // Hiding constructor
  }

  public void Log(string message)
  {
    Console.WriteLine("{0}: {1}", DateTime.Now, message);
  }
}
```

And instructing the binding to always use the provided instance rather than every time creating a new instance of ConsoleLogger. We can achieve this by using the ToConstant method:

```
kernel.Bind<ILogger>().ToConstant(ConsoleLogger.Instance);
```

However, if we make a singleton type like this, we will draw some limitations to our class. For example, we won't be able to unit test, it because it doesn't have a default constructor.

Using lifetime management of Ninject, we will be able to have singleton objects without having to make their type singleton. All we need to do is to instruct Ninject to treat the given type as singleton:

```
kernel.Bind<ILogger>().To<ConsoleLogger>().InSingletonScope();
```

Now, what if we decide to change the scope of MailServerConfig to singleton as well? There is no binding definition for this type because Ninject already knows how to resolve it. Such classes are actually bound to themselves. Although Ninject doesn't require us to register such types, if we need to change their scope, we can explicitly define their binding in order to set their lifetime scope:

```
kernel.Bind<MailServerConfig>().ToSelf().InSingletonScope();
```

Thread scope

If we define a binding in Thread scope, only one instance of the given type will be created per thread. The object lifetime is as long as the lifetime of the underlying Thread object.

The following test asserts equality of instances created by Ninject in the same thread:

```
[Test]
public void ReturnsTheSameInstancesInOneThread()
{
  using (var kernel = new StandardKernel())
  {
    kernel.Bind<object>().ToSelf().InThreadScope();
    var instance1 = kernel.Get<object>();
    var instance2 = kernel.Get<object>();
    Assert.AreEqual(instance1, instance2);
  }
}
```

In the previous example, we instructed Ninject to bind the type object to itself and create new instances of object per thread. Then, we asked Ninject to return two instances of type object in the same thread and tested their equality. The test succeeded.

The following test demonstrates inequality of the instances created from the same type but in different threads:

```
[Test]
public void ReturnsDifferentInstancesInDifferentThreads()
{
  var kernel = new StandardKernel();
  kernel.Bind<object>().ToSelf().InThreadScope();
  var instance1 = kernel.Get<object>();
  new Thread(() =>
  {
    var instance2 = kernel.Get<object>();
    Assert.AreNotEqual(instance1, instance2);
    kernel.Dispose();
  }).Start();
}
```

This time we got the second instance in another thread. Ninject detects that the calling thread is changed, and this is the first time that an instance of object is being requested in this new thread. So, it creates a new instance rather than returning the existing one. Finally, we asserted inequality of the created instances.

Request scope

Request scope is useful in web applications when we need to get a single instance of a type from Ninject as long as we are handling the same request. Once the request is processed and a new request arrives, Ninject creates a new instance of the type and keeps it until the end of the request processing. Note that Request scope behaves like Transient scope outside of a web request (for example, during startup) or in non-web applications.

The following code shows how to change the scope of the `MailService` type, so that we get a new instance only for new web requests, and keep the existing instance during the current request:

```
kernel.Bind<MailServerConfig>().ToSelf().InRequestScope();
```

The `InRequestScope` method is not available unless we add a reference to the `Ninject.Web.Common` library, which makes sense only in web applications. *Chapter 4, Ninject in Action*, will discuss web applications in detail.

Custom scope

Custom scope lets us define our own scopes in which to keep an instance of a type unique. As long as reference of the object returned by the provided call-back is the same, Ninject returns the same instance of the type which is created in this scope. Once reference of the returned object is changed, a new instance of the given type will be created. The created instance is kept in the cache until the returned scope object is garbage collected. As soon as the scope object is garbage collected, all the object instances created by Ninject will be released from the cache and disposed.

The following test shows how to define a custom scope which monitors the current user:

```
[Test]
public void ReturnsTheSameInstancesForAUser()
{
using (var kernel = new StandardKernel())
    {
        kernel.Bind<object>().ToSelf().InScope(ctx =>User.Current);
        User.Current = new User();
        var instance1 = kernel.Get<object>();
        User.Current.Name = "Foo";
        var instance2 = kernel.Get<object>();
        Assert.AreEqual(instance1, instance2);
    }
}
```

The User class has the following structure, and the Current static property is supposed to be populated with the current User:

```
class User
{
  public string Name { get; set; }
  public static User Current { get; set; }
}
```

Although User.Current is modified in the previous example, the reference is still the same (User.Current is still referring to the same object), so the scope is not changed. As the test shows, we are getting the same instance of object every time we call kernel.Get<object>().

```
[Test]
public void ReturnsDifferentInstancesForDifferentUsers()
{
  using (var kernel = new StandardKernel())
  {
    kernel.Bind<object>().ToSelf().InScope(ctx =>User.Current);

    User.Current = new User();
    var instance1 = kernel.Get<object>();
    User.Current = new User();
    var instance2 = kernel.Get<object>();
    Assert.AreNotEqual(instance1, instance2);
  }
}
```

Since we have changed the user, the scope is changed, and kernel is returning a different instance in the new scope.

You may have noticed that the call-back function provides an argument of type IContext which is named ctx. This object provides information about the binding context which can be used in order to create the scope object. The Context object will be discussed in *Chapter 3, Meeting Real-world Requirements*, and we are not going to use it at the moment. Just keep in mind that returning anything from the provided context as scope should be handled with extra care. For example, returning the context itself as scope would result in a memory leak. Although a new instance is returned, it will be kept in the cache forever.

Custom scope is the most flexible and powerful scope, and it is also possible to implement other scopes using Custom scope.

The following example shows how to implement Thread scope using Custom scope:

```
kernel.Bind<object>().ToSelf().InScope(ctx=>Thread.CurrentThread);
```

The following snippet implements Request scope using Custom scope:

```
kernel.Bind<object>().ToSelf().InScope(ctx=>HttpContext.Current);
```

We can always ask kernel to dispose of an object whose lifetime is being managed by Ninject:

```
var myObject = kernel.Get<MyService>();
..
kernel.Release(myObject);
```

> Ninject also has an extension called Named Scope, which adds some additional scopes other than the common ones we addressed here. For more information, see Named Scope on Ninject official wiki: `github.com/ninject/ninject.extensions.namedscope/wiki`

Ninject modules

As our application grows, the list of service registrations gets longer, and it would be difficult to manage this list. Ninject modules are a good way to segregate our type bindings into distinct groups of bindings, which can be easily organized into separate files. Minimum requirement for a class to be accepted as a Ninject module is to implement the `INinjectModule` interface. Implementing this interface requires us to implement three methods and two properties each time we need to create a module. It is a good idea to implement this interface as an abstract class once, and extend it whenever we need to create a Ninject module. The good news is that Ninject has already implemented this abstract class, which is named `NinjectModule`.

Here is how to register our `MailService` classes in a module:

```
class MailServiceModule: NinjectModule
{
public override void Load()
  {
    Bind<ILogger>().To<ConsoleLogger>().InSingletonScope();
    Bind<MailServerConfig>().ToSelf().InRequestScope();
  }
}
```

After declaring our modules, we need to load them into kernel so that Ninject can use them to resolve the registered types. Put this code into the `Main` method:

```
using (var kernel = new StandardKernel(new MailServiceModule()))
{
  var mailService = kernel.Get<MailService>();
  mailService.SendMail("someone@somewhere.com", "Hello", null);
}
```

The following code shows how to load multiple modules in a single Ninject kernel:

```
var kernel = newStandardKernel(newModule1(), newModule2(), … );
```

We can also load all of the Ninject modules defined in an application at the same time using the following code:

```
kernel.Load(AppDomain.CurrentDomain.GetAssemblies());
```

In this case, Ninject looks in all assemblies for the public classes which have implemented the `INinjectModule` interface to load type registrations. The next example will show how to load modules dynamically.

XML configuration

Ninject supports both code-based and XML configuration. An XML module is like a code module that consists of a list of type registrations via Ninject binding. All bindings can be defined in a single XML document or segregated into multiple documents. The only advantage of using XML modules over code modules is that once we have composed such a document, we can still change our type registrations without having to recompile any part of the application. However, XML modules are not as powerful as code modules; so it is recommended to use code modules unless we need this feature. Even in this case, we can only include those bindings for which we need to change the configuration at runtime in our XML module and keep other bindings in code modules.

How to use XML configuration

In order to use XML configuration, we need to add a reference to the Ninject XML extension. It can be added either by installing `Ninject.Extensions.Xml` via `NuGet` package manager or by downloading the binary files from GitHub.

The next step is to add one or more XML documents to our project to contain our type registrations. Keep in mind that these files should be published along with your application. So don't forget to set their `Copy to Output Directory` property to `Copy if newer`.

An XML document should look like the following configuration:

```xml
<module name="moduleName">
    <bind service="Namespace.IService1, AssemblyName"
        to="Namespace.ConcreteService1, AssemblyName" />
    <bind service="Namespace.IService2, AssemblyName"
        to="Namespace.ConcreteService2, AssemblyName"
        Scope="singleton"/>
</module>
```

Each binding element contains at least two attributes:

- `Service`: It represents the service type, which is usually an interface or an abstract type
- `To`: It represents the concrete type, which is an implementation of the service type

The types should be defined as assembly qualified names which should contain namespace, type name, and assembly name. For more information about assembly qualified names, check the following MSDN page:

`http://msdn.microsoft.com/en-us/library/system.type.assemblyqualifiedname.aspx`

The next example will show how to use the XML configuration in a DI project.

In this example we are going to create a project which contains two encryptor classes, each of which implements a particular encryption algorithm. Both classes implement a common interface named `IEncryptor` which is referenced in the consumer. We will configure the application to use one of the encryptors dynamically. This configuration can be changed later and we will see how to instruct the application to swap the encryptors without being recompiled.

Open Visual Studio and add references to Ninject and the `Ninject.Extensions.Xml` libraries. Then, add the `IEncryptor` interface as follows:

```
public interface IEncryptor
{
   string Encrypt(string str);
}
```

The next step is to implement this interface and create our concrete services. Let's start with `ReverseEncryptor`. The encryption algorithm is to reverse the given string:

```csharp
public class ReverseEncryptor : IEncryptor
{
  public string Encrypt(string str)
  {
    var charArray = str.Reverse().ToArray();
    return new string(charArray);
  }
}
```

Now we are going to implement the ShiftEncryptor class, which implements another algorithm. This class shifts up each character code to encrypt the given string:

```csharp
public class ShiftEncryptor : IEncryptor
{
  public string Encrypt(string str)
  {
    var charArray = str.Select(c => (char)(c + 1)).ToArray();
    return new string(charArray);
  }
}
```

Now, let's add a new XML document to our project and register one of our concrete encryptors like this:

```xml
<module name="encryptorModule">
<bind service="Samples.Encryption.IEncryptor, Encryptors"
to="Samples.Encryption.ShiftEncryptor, Encryptors" />
</module>
```

Note that the name of our assembly is Encryptors, and our classes are declared in Samples.Encryption namespace. Don't forget to set the Copy to Output Directory property of this file to Copy if newer, so that it can be copied to the output directory automatically.

The next step is to load the XML module in the kernel. We can put this code in the Main method of our application:

```csharp
var kernel = new StandardKernel();
kernel.Load("typeRegistrations.xml");
```

The final step is to consume the service using the following code:

```csharp
var encryptor = kernel.Get<IEncryptor>();
Console.WriteLine(encryptor.Encrypt("Hello"));
Console.ReadKey();
```

Running the application leads to the following output:

```
Ifmmp
```

At this step, we don't need Visual Studio anymore; we can navigate to the output directory of our application and just change the service type in the configuration file to `"Samples.Encryption.IEncryptor, Encryptors"`. Note that we don't need to recompile the application.

Running the application should result in the following output:

```
olleH
```

We have dynamically replaced the Encryptor service in our application using XML configuration.

The following code snippet shows how to load multiple XML modules into kernel. The first overload accepts individual paths to the XML configuration files. The paths can either be relative to the output directory or start from the file system root:

```
kernel.Load("module1.xml","module2.xml","module3.xml");
```

We can also use `"*"` as a wildcard character to address any path that matches the declared pattern. In the following example, the kernel loads all of the XML files from the same directory of the executing assembly:

```
kernel.Load("*.xml");
```

In the next example, the kernel loads the XML files which are located in a directory named `Modules`, located in the application directory:

```
kernel.Load("Modules/*.xml");
```

Convention over configuration

It is not difficult to register a few service types, one by one in a small application. But what about a production application with hundreds of services which should be wired to their implementations?

Convention-based configuration allows us to bind a group of services using a convention rather than defining individual bindings for each of them. For example, you can simply ask Ninject to bind all components to their base interfaces like this:

```
kernel.Bind(r => r
  .FromThisAssembly()
  .SelectAllClasses()
  .BindAllInterfaces());
```

In order to take advantage of the Convention based configuration, we should add refererence to the Ninject's Conventions extension. We can either use NuGet to install `Ninject.Extensions.Conventions` or download the binary file from GitHub. We also need to add `Ninject.Extensions.Conventions` to the using section of our code to make the previous syntax available.

As the syntax indicates, registering a convention-based binding at least consists of the following steps:

1. Selecting the assembly or assemblies which contain the concrete components.
2. Selecting the concrete components within the selected assemblies.
3. Selecting the service types relative to the selected components.

One thing that may look weird in this syntax is that we are selecting the concrete components prior to the service types, which is in reverse order compared to the ordinary binding registration.

The first reason is that each implementation can be bound to many service types, whereas each service type cannot be bound to more than one implementation. The syntax is actually telling Ninject to bind each selected implementation to its relevant service types, which can address many services. But if we asked Ninject to bind each selected service type to its relevant implementation, no more than one binding per service type would be valid and hence, created.

The second reason is that this syntax forces to select the components first and then only select those services which can be bound to the selected components. This way, it is not possible to select the service types for which there is no implementation. Note that the service selection clause doesn't allow us to select every desired service types. We can only select services relative to the selected components (for example, their base classes).

The third reason is that it is possible to locate the service types based on a given implementation, because each component has a reference to its base service types. That is why we select assemblies only for components and not for the service types. But a given service type doesn't have any idea about its implementations.

Selecting the assemblies

The first step to register a convention is to project the assemblies which contain the component types. It can either be the current assembly or an external one.

Here are some of the methods which can be used to identify an assembly:

- `FromThisAssembly()`: It selects the assembly that contains the current line of code.

- `From(params Assembly[] assemblies)`: It selects the specified assemblies.

- `FromAssemblyContaining<SomeType>()`: It selects the assembly that contains the specified type.

In case not all of the components are in a single assembly, the `Join` syntax can be used to select multiple assemblies:

```
kernel.Bind(x => x
    .FromAssemblyContaining<CustomersService>()
    .SelectAllClasses()
    .Join
    .FromAssemblyContaining<MessageProvider>()
    .SelectAllClasses()
    .BindAllInterfaces());
```

Generally, only public types are exposed in the projected assemblies. In order to also include the non-public types, we should explicitly declare this by using the `IncludingNonePublicTypes()` method after the assembly selection clause:

```
    .FromAssemblyContaining<CustomersService>()
    .IncludingNonePublicTypes()
    .SelectAllClasses()
    .BindAllInterfaces());
```

Selecting the components

The second step is to select the components to which the bindings are going to be registered. We can use either the `SelectAllClasses()` method to select all non-abstract classes or the `Select(Func<Type, bool> filter)` method to select any desired types. The following example shows how to select all classes whose names start with word "customer":

```
kernel.Bind(r => r
    .FromThisAssembly()
    .Select(t =>t.Name.StartsWith("Customer"))
    .BindBase());
```

Filtering the selected components

We don't have to select all types within the selected assembly. It is possible to apply conditions to filter the results. The following code binds only those classes which are in the `"Northwind.Controllers"` namespace to their base type:

```
kernel.Bind(x => x
  .FromThisAssembly()
  .SelectAllClasses()
  .InNamespaces("Northwind.Controllers")
  .BindBase());
```

Explicit inclusion and exclusion

We can also exclude or include some types explicitly to make the final component list exactly match our requirements using the Exclude or Include methods.

Selecting service types

Now that we have projected the concrete components, we should select their corresponding service types to participate in the binding. We can use one of the following methods to indicate the service types relative to each projected component:

- `BindAllInterfaces()`: It binds all the interfaces of the selected component to the selected component.

- `BindBase()`: It binds the base type of the selected components to the current component.

- `BindDefaultInterface()`: Binds the default interface of the given types to the type. The default interface is the interface with the same name as the type. For example, `ICustomerSerive` is the default interface for `CustomerService`.

- `BindDefaultInterfaces()`: It binds the default interfaces of the given types to the type. Default interfaces for a type are all of the interfaces that the type's name ends with their names. For example, `IRepository` and `ICustomerRepository` are both default interfaces for `SqlCustomerRepository`.

- `BindSingleInterface()`: It requires that the given type has exactly one interface. In this case, this interface is bound to the type. If the type has no or several interfaces then no binding is added.

- `BindToSelf()`: It binds the type to itself.

- `BindSelection(ServiceSelector selector)`: It binds the selected interfaces to the type.

- `BindUsingRegex(string pattern)`: It binds the interfaces of the current type matching the given regular expression to the type.

Configuring the Bindings

Once a binding is created, we can configure it in the same way we configure ordinary bindings:

```
kernel.Bind(x => x
    .FromThisAssembly()
    .SelectAllClasses()
    .BindAllInterfaces()
    .Configure(b=>b.InSingletonScope()));
```

Additionally, we have access to each component type in the corresponding binding configuration. The following method shows how to define Named bindings using the component's type name:

```
kernel.Bind(x => x
    .FromAssemblyContaining<MessageProvider>()
    .SelectAllClasses()
    .BindAllInterfaces()
    .Configure((b, c) =>b.Named(c.Name)));
```

We can also configure certain types individually using the `ConfigureFor<T>` method. In the following example, all the repository classes are given a connection string and configured to live in a Singleton scope. `SqlCustomerRepository` is also getting the same connection string, but its scope configuration is overridden to be `InThreadScope`:

```
kernel.Bind(x => x
    .FromThisAssembly()
    .SelectAllClasses()
    .InheritedFrom<IRepository>()
    .BindAllInterfaces()
    .Configure(b =>b.InSingletonScope ()
.WithConstructorArgument("connectionString", ApplicationSettings.
ConnectionString))
    .ConfigureFor<SqlCustomerRepository>(b =>b.InThreadScope()));
```

Summary

Ninject uses its binding system to map abstract services to concrete types. The core object of Ninject to which we give a service type and get the concrete service is Ninject kernel. Ninject uses the object scopes to deal with Lifetime of the created objects. We can use the predefined scopes or create our custom scopes to define the lifetime of objects created by Ninject. Ninject supports both code-based and XML-based configurations for registering service types. Although XML modules can be modified without having to compile the application, code modules are more powerful and recommended. Instead of registering each service individually, we usually use conventions to register a group of services at a time.

3
Meeting Real-world Requirements

This chapter starts with some patterns and antipatterns which should be considered while using Ninject. We will go through the advanced features of Ninject, and also some examples to see how Ninject can meet real-world requirements. By the end of this chapter, the user is expected to know almost all the significant features of Ninject.

The topics covered in this chapter are as follows:

- DI patterns and antipatterns
- Multi binding and contextual binding
- Custom providers
- Dynamic factories

DI patterns and antipatterns

Dependencies can be injected in a consumer class using different patterns and injecting them into a constructor is just one of them. While there are some patterns that can be followed for injecting dependencies, there are also some patterns that are recommended to be avoided, as they usually lead to undesirable results. In this section, we will examine only those patterns and antipatterns that are somehow relevant to Ninject features. However, a comprehensive study of them can be found in Mark Seemann's book, Dependency Injection in .NET.

Constructor Injection

Constructor Injection is the most common and recommended pattern for injecting dependencies in a class. Generally this pattern should always be used as the primary injection pattern unless we have to use other ones. In this pattern, a list of all class dependencies should be introduced in the constructor.

The question is what if the class has more than one constructor. Although Ninject's strategy for selecting constructor is customizable, its default behavior is selecting the constructor with more parameters, provided all of them are resolvable by Ninject. So, although in the following code the second constructor introduces more parameters, Ninject will select the first one if it cannot resolve IService2 and it will even use the default constructor if IService1 is not registered either. But if both dependencies are registered and resolvable, Ninject will select the second constructor because it has more parameters:

```
public class Consumer
{
    private readonly IService1 dependency1;
    private readonly IService2 dependency2;
    public Consumer(IService1 dependency1)
    {
        this.dependency1 = dependency1;
    }

    public Consumer(IService1 dependency1, IService2 dependency2)
    {
        this.dependency1 = dependency1;
        this.dependency2 = dependency2;
    }
}
```

If the preceding class had another constructor with two resolvable parameters, Ninject would throw an ActivationException exception notifying that several constructors had the same priority.

There are two approaches to override this default behavior and explicitly select a constructor. The first approach is to indicate the desired constructor in a binding as follows:

```
Bind<Consumer>().ToConstructor(arg =>
    new Consumer(arg.Inject<IService1>()));
```

In the preceding example, we explicitly selected the first constructor. Using the Inject<T> method that the arg argument provides, we requested Ninject to resolve IService1 in order to be injected into the specified constructor.

The second method is to indicate the desired constructor using the `[Inject]` attribute:

```
[Inject]
public Consumer(IService1 dependency1)
{
    this.dependency1 = dependency1;
}
```

In the preceding example, we applied the Ninject's `[Inject]` attribute on the first constructor to explicitly specify that we need to initialize the class by injecting dependencies into this constructor; even though the second constructor has more parameters and the default strategy of Ninject would be to select the second one. Note that applying this attribute on more than one constructor will result in the `ActivationException`.

Ninject is highly customizable and it is even possible to substitute the default `[Inject]` attribute with another one, so that we don't need to add reference to the Ninject library from our consumer classes just because of an attribute:

```
kernel.Settings.Set("InjectAttribute",typeof(MyAttribute));
```

Initializer methods and properties

Apart from constructor injection, Ninject supports the injection of dependencies using initializer methods and property setters. We can specify as many methods and properties as required using the `[Inject]` attribute to inject dependencies. Although the dependencies will be injected to them as soon as the class is constructed, it is not possible to predict in which order they will receive their dependencies. The following code shows how to specify a property for injection:

```
[Inject]
public IService Service
{
    get { return dependency;  }
    set { dependency = value; }
}
```

Here is an example of injecting dependencies using an injector method:

```
[Inject]
public void Setup(IService dependency)
{
    this.dependency = dependency;
}
```

Note that only `public` members and constructors will be injected and even the internals will be ignored unless Ninject is configured to inject nonpublic members.

In Constructor Injection, the constructor is a single point where we can consume all of the dependencies as soon as the class is activated. But when we use initializer methods the dependencies will be injected via multiple points in an unpredictable order, so we cannot decide in which method all of the dependencies will be ready to consume. In order to solve this problem, Ninject offers the `IInitializable` interface. This interface has an `Initialize` method which will be called once all of the dependencies have been injected:

```
public class Consumer:IInitializable
{
    private IService1 dependency1;
    private IService2 dependency2;

    [Inject]
    public IService Service1
    {
        get { return dependency1;  }
        set { dependency1 = value; }
    }

    [Inject]
    public IService Service2
    {
        get { return dependency2;  }
        set { dependency2 = value; }
    }

    public void Initialize()
    {
        // Consume all dependencies here
    }
}
```

Although Ninject supports injection using properties and methods, Constructor Injection should be the superior approach. First of all, Constructor Injection makes the class more reusable, because a list of all class dependencies are visible, while in the initializer property or method the user of the class should investigate all of the class members or go through the class documentations (if any), to discover its dependencies.

Initialization of the class is easier while using Constructor Injection because all the dependencies get injected at the same time and we can easily consume them at the same place where the constructor initializes the class. As we have seen in the preceding examples the only case where the backing fields could be readonly was in the Constructor Injection scenario. As the readonly fields are initializable only in the constructor, we need to make them writable to be able to use initializer methods and properties. This can lead to potential mutation of backing fields.

Service Locator

Service Locator is a design pattern introduced by *Martin Fowler* regarding which there have been some controversies. Although it can be useful in particular circumstances, it is generally considered as an antipattern and preferably should be avoided. Ninject can easily be misused as a Service Locator if we are not familiar to this pattern. The following example demonstrates misusing the Ninject kernel as a Service Locator rather than a DI container:

```
public class Consumer
{
    public void Consume()
    {
        var kernel = new StandardKernel();
        var depenency1 = kernel.Get<IService1>();
        var depenency2 = kernel.Get<IService2>();
        ...
    }
}
```

There are two significant downsides with the preceding code. The first one is that although we are using a DI container, we are not at all implementing DI. The class is tied to the Ninject kernel while it is not really a dependency of this class. This class and all of its prospective consumers will always have to drag their unnecessary dependency on the kernel object and Ninject library. On the other hand, the real dependencies of class (`IService1` and `IService2`) are invisible from the consumers, and this reduces its reusability. Even if we change the design of this class to the following one, the problems still exist:

```
public class Consumer
{
    private readonly IKernel kernel;
    public Consumer(IKernel kernel)
    {
```

```
            this.kernel = kernel;
    }

    public void Consume()
    {
        var depenency1 = kernel.Get<IService1>();
        var depenency2 = kernel.Get<IService2>();
        ...
    }
}
```

The preceding class still depends on the Ninject library while it doesn't have to and its actual dependencies are still invisible to its consumers. It can easily be refactored using the Constructor Injection pattern:

```
public Consumer(IService1 dependency1, IService2 dependency2)
{
    this.dependency1 = dependency1;
    this.dependency2 = dependency2;
}
```

Multi binding and contextual binding

In the previous chapter, we saw how Ninject can resolve dependency types in single binding situations, that is, each service type is bound only to a single implementation type. However, there are situations where we need to bind an abstract service type to multiple implementations, which is called as multi binding. Multi binding has two scenarios. The first one is the plugin model implementation and the other one is contextual binding, which we will discuss in this section.

Implementing the plugin model

The plugin model allows an application to be extremely extensible without modifying its source code. In the following example, we will implement a Music Player application, which uses codec plugins in order to support different music formats. The application comes out with two built-in codecs, and it is possible to add more plugin codecs and extend the formats that our player application supports. Please note that as we try to keep the application as simple as possible, many complexities and details will not be implemented.

Let's start by defining the interface of our codec plugin as follows:

```
public interface ICodec
{
    string Name { get; }
    bool CanDecode(string extension);
    Stream Decode(Stream inStream);
}
```

The next step is to implement our pluggable player. What makes the player extensible is that it depends on a sequence of the ICodec objects, rather than a certain number of concrete codecs:

```
public class Player
{
    private readonly ICodec[] codecs;

    // Note that the constructor parameter is not a single ICodec.
    public Player(IEnumerable<ICodec> codecs)
    {
        this.codecs = codecs.ToArray();
    }
}
```

Then we will add a Play method to our Player class as follows:

```
public void Play(FileInfo fileInfo)
{
    ICodec supportingCodec = FindCodec(fileInfo.Extension);
    using (var rawStream = fileInfo.OpenRead())
    {
        var decodedStream = supportingCodec.Decode(rawStream);
        PlayStream(decodedStream);
    }
}
```

This method accepts a FileInfo object and after finding a suitable codec, it decodes and plays the given file. We can assume that our player has a PlayStream method which can play decoded streams.

Now, let's implement the `FindCodec` method as follows:

```
private ICodec FindCodec(string extension)
{
    foreach (ICodec codec in codecs)
        if (codec.CanDecode(extension))
            return codec;

    throw new Exception("File type not supported.");
}
```

`FindCodec` calls the `CanDecode` method of each codec object to find a codec which supports the given file extension. If it cannot find any codecs suitable for the given file type, it throws an error. One of the things that we need to keep in mind is that none of our concrete codecs have been resolved before this `foreach` loop.

 Ninject doesn't resolve the types within a sequence unless the sequence is enumerated.

The final step is to add a convention to the entry point of our UI layer, which is a console application in this case. Open the `Main` method and add the following lines:

```
using (var kernel = new StandardKernel())
{
    kernel.Bind(b => b.FromAssembliesMatching("*")
                    .SelectAllClasses()
                    .InheritedFrom<ICodec>()
                    .BindAllInterfaces());
}
```

The preceding convention instructs Ninject to register all implementations of the `ICodec` interface automatically without having to declare individual bindings for them.

Since the `ICodec` type is bound to multiple implementations, it can only be resolved to a sequence of objects rather than a single object. So, resolving `ICodec` with the following constructor will result in a runtime exception:

```
public Consumer(ICodec codec){}
```

The result is the same if we execute the following code:

```
ICodec codec = Kernel.Get<ICodec>();
```

In both cases, Ninject will try to resolve ICodec, but it will find more than one concrete type for it. Instead of Get<T>, we can call the GetAll<T> method to get all the implementations of ICodec. The following code shows the names of all supported codecs:

```
IEnumerable<ICodec> codecs = kernel.GetAll<ICodec>();
foreach (ICodec codec in codecs)
    System.Console.WriteLine(codec.Name);
```

Now, any assemblies that have an implementation of ICodec and are located in the root directory of our application will be recognized as a codec plugin by our Player application. Our application does not even need to have a reference to the codec project.

 The code sample and built-in codec plugins can be downloaded from the publisher's website.

Contextual binding

Since in the plugin model each service type can be mapped to multiple implementations, the binding engine doesn't need to make any decision about which implementation to return; because the kernel is supposed to return all of them. Contextual binding, however, is a multi-binding scenario in which the kernel has to choose one implementation among multiple provided types based on a given condition.

In the following example, we will implement a data migration application which can migrate data from a SQL database to an XML datafile. It is going to have a presentation layer, a business layer, and a data access layer.

Our SQL database is Northwind which exists as a sample database with the SQL server installation package. In order to keep this sample clean and simple, we use the Shippers table, which contains only two fields: Shipper ID and Company Name.

We add a class library project to our solution to implement the business layer. The only business model will be the Shipper class. It has only the following members:

```
public int ShipperID { get; set; }
public string CompanyName { get; set; }
```

The next step is to implement our `ShippersService` class. It should contain a method for migrating data from our source repository, which is a SQL database to the target repository, which is an XML datafile:

```
public void MigrateShippers()
{
    foreach (Shipper shipper in sourceRepository.GetShippers())
        targetRepository.AddShipper(shipper);
}
```

What should the type of these repositories be and where should they come from? The answer to these questions can turn this application into a loosely coupled maintainable application or a tightly coupled hard to maintain one. The easiest way may be to create an `XmlRepository` and `SQLRepository` and then instantiate them in the `ShippersService` class as follows:

```
// The following code leads to a tightly coupled code
var sourceRepository = new ShippersSqlRepository();
var targetRepository = new ShippersXmlRepository();
```

This way, we will make our service dependent of these two concrete repositories and tighten our business layer to our data access layer. It would not be possible to modify or replace the data access without modifying the business layer and recompiling the application. Although our application layers may look like being separated, they are actually so tightly coupled that it is not easily maintainable.

The solution is to create our `ShippersService` class based on an abstraction of the repositories which can be defined in the business layer, rather than the concrete repositories which will be implemented in the data access layer. Let's define this abstraction using the following interface in our business layer:

```
public interface IShippersRepository
{
    IEnumerable<Shipper> GetShippers();
    void AddShipper(Shipper shipper);
}
```

Now we can use this interface rather than the concrete repositories the `ShippersService` class as follows:

```
public class ShippersService
{
    ...
```

```
    public ShippersService(IShippersRepository sourceRepository,
IShippersRepository targetRepository)
    {
        this.sourceRepository = sourceRepository;
        this.targetRepository = targetRepository;
    }

    public void MigrateShippers()
    {
        foreach (var shipper in sourceRepository.GetShippers())
            targetRepository.AddShipper(shipper);
    }
}
```

The ShippersService class is now highly reusable. It can migrate Shipper instances not only from SQL to XML, but also between any types of data sources as long as they implement IShippersRepository. The interesting thing is that we can easily migrate data in reverse direction without modifying our ShippersService class or data access layer.

We know that Ninject will inject concrete repositories into the constructor of the ShippersService class. But wait for a second. The type of both parameters is IShippersRepository. How will Ninject understand which concrete type should be injected into which parameter? Contextual binding is the answer to this question. Let's go through different resolution approaches one by one.

Named binding

This is the simplest approach in which we can assign names to both our binding and our target parameters so that Ninject can decide which binding should be used for which target. We need to insert names on targets as well as their corresponding bindings:

```
public ShippersService(
    [Named("Source")]IShippersRepository sourceRepository,
    [Named("Target")]IShippersRepository targetRepository)
```

The following code shows the type registration section in our presentation layer, which is a console application:

```
Bind<IShippersRepository>()
.To<ShippersSqlRepository>().Named("Source");
Bind<IShippersRepository>()
.To<ShippersXmlRepository>().Named("Target");
```

Now that we have distinguished the different implementations of
`IShippersRepository` with names, it is also possible to get them from the `kernel`
object using the following syntax:

```
kernel.Get<IShippersRepository>("Source");
```

However, resolving instances in this way is not recommended because in this way,
Ninject will be misused as a means for implementing the Service Locator antipattern.

> Once a binding is named, this name can also be used to address
> any subsequent dependencies of the registered types.

Resolving metadata

In this approach, each bindings is provided with some metadata which can
be evaluated while resolving the types. The following code shows how to
set metadata:

```
Bind<IShippersRepository>().To<ShippersSqlRepository>()
    .WithMetadata("IsSource", true);
Bind<IShippersRepository>().To<ShippersXmlRepository>()
    .WithMetadata("IsSource", false);
```

One way of associating targets with their corresponding bindings is by defining
a custom `ConstraintAttribute` class. This is an abstract class which provides a
method for matching the attributed target with its desired binding. The following
code shows how to define such an attribute:

```
public class IsSourceAttribute : ConstraintAttribute
{
    private readonly bool isSource;
    public IsSourceAttribute(bool isSource)
    {
        this.isSource = isSource;
    }

    public override bool Matches (Ninject.Planning.Bindings.
IBindingMetadata metadata)
    {
        return metadata.Has("IsSource")
            && metadata.Get<bool>("IsSource") == isSource
    }
}
```

Now, we can apply this attribute to the targets to associate them with their corresponding bindings:

```
public ShippersService([IsSource(true)]IShippersRepository
sourceRepository, [IsSource(false)]IShippersRepository
targetRepository)
{
    this.sourceRepository = sourceRepository;
    this.targetRepository = targetRepository;
}
```

We can provide as many metadata as required to our binding for being used while resolving the associated services:

```
Bind<IService>().To<Component>()
.WithMetadata("Key1", value1)
.WithMetadata("Key2", value2)
.WithMetadata("Key3", value3);
```

We can also provide as many `Constraint` attributes as needed on a binding target, as shown in the following code:

```
public Consumer(
[Constraint1(value1, value2), Constraint2(value), Constraint3]
IService dependency)
{
}
```

Please keep in mind that named binding scenario is also implemented using metadata. The following code shows how to implement a custom constraint attribute which can resolve named bindings based on a matching pattern rather than the exact name:

```
public class NamedLikeAttribute : ConstraintAttribute
{
    private readonly string pattern;
    public NamedLike(string namePattern)
    {
        this.pattern = namePattern;
    }

    public override bool Matches(IBindingMetadata metadata)
    {
        return Regex.IsMatch(metadata.Name, pattern);
    }
}
```

Given a pattern, the preceding attribute can be applied to the target. The binding name then will be evaluated using a Regular Expression to determine whether or not the name matches the given pattern. The following code shows how to use this attribute:

```
public Consumer([NamedLike(@"source\w+") dependency)
{
    ...
}
```

In order to understand how metadata can help Ninject resolve types, we need to know how binding targets are associated with bindings. The following diagram shows a simplified demonstration of this relationship:

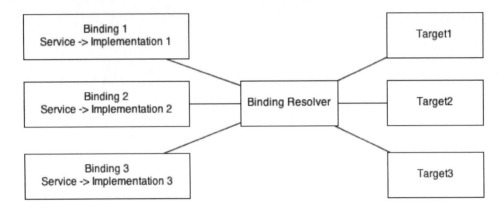

Ninject Kernel uses different components to resolve types, and one of them is **Binding Resolver**. Although Binding Resolver refers to a group of Ninject components rather than a single one, we can think of it as a single component for now to keep things simple. When Ninject is asked for resolving a service type, Binding Resolver will be provided with all of the registered bindings as well as a Request object which contains information about the target for which a resolution is requested. Binding information includes binding metadata and target information contains attributes set on the target. Binding Resolver examines all of the targets using this information in order to find their matching bindings. Whenever it detects a constraint attribute on a target, it executes the Matches method of that attribute across all of the bindings to find the matching binding. Once the matching binding is found, it is easy to get the concrete type from that binding.

Attribute-based binding

Although Named binding is simple to use and metadata is flexible and powerful, both the approaches require library of the dependent classes to have a reference to the Ninject library. Another downside of these two solutions is that they both rely on strings, which are error prone. One can easily mistype the names or metadata keys without being warned by the compiler.

The following code shows how to use this technique without referencing the Ninject library:

```
public class SourceAttribute : Attribute{}
public class TargetAttribute : Attribute{}
```

These attributes then can be applied to the target parameters as follows:

```
public ShippersService([Source]IShippersRepository sourceRepository,
[Target]IShippersRepository targetRepository)
```

Now, we need to register our bindings using the following code:

```
Bind<IShippersRepository>().To<ShippersSqlRepository>()
    .WhenTargetHas<SourceAttribute>()

Bind<IShippersRepository>().To<ShippersXmlRepository>()
    .WhenTargetHas<TargetAttribute>()
```

Not only can we apply these attributes to parameters, but we can also apply them to the class itself or to the other injected members, for example, the constructor itself.

The following binding shows how to make a binding conditional based on an attribute on the consuming class:

```
Bind<IService>().To<MyService>().WhenClassHas<MyAttribute>();
```

Here is the consuming class:

```
[MyAttribute]
Public class Consumer {...}
```

The following code shows how to make a binding conditional based on an attribute on an injected class member:

```
Bind<IService>().To<MyService>().WhenClassHas<MyAttribute>();
```

This is how we can apply such an attribute to the constructor:

```
[MyAttribute]
public Consumer(IServive service) { ... }
```

A class member can be the constructor itself, or it can even be another method, or an injected property. We will talk about these kinds of binding later in this chapter.

Target-based conditions

Another way of deciding which binding to use is target-based conditions. Ninject offers several helpers which can restrict the number of matching bindings for a target based on the type of its container. The following example shows a scenario to which this approach applies.

In this example, we have two service classes named `SourceShipperService` and `TargetShipperService`, both of which depend on `IShippersRepository`.

Here is the structure of our service classes:

```
public class SourceShipperService
{
    public SourceShipperService(IShippersRepository repository)
    {  ...  }
}

public class TargetShipperService
{
    public TargetShipperService(IShippersRepository repository)
    {  ...  }
}
```

In order to tell Ninject which concrete repository should be injected into which service, we can base our condition on the service type itself rather than any attribute or metadata.

The following code shows how to register our types in such a way that instances of `ShippersXmlRepository` and `ShippersSqlRepository` respectively get injected into `SourceShipperService` and `TargetShipperService`:

```
Bind<IShippersRepository>().To<ShippersXmlRepository>()
    .WhenInjectedInto<SourceShipperService>();
Bind<IShippersRepository>().To<ShippersSqlRepository>()
    .WhenInjectedInto<TargetShipperService>();
```

Note that the `WhenInjectedInto<T>` method will match even if the target class is a subtype of `T`. If we mean exactly the given type, we should use the following alternative method:

```
Bind<IShippersRepository>().To<ShippersSqlRepository>()
    .WhenInjectedExactlyInto<TargetShipperService>();
```

Generic helper

As we have seen, most of the preceding approaches take advantage of the helper methods whose names follow the `Whenxxx` pattern. All of these methods are specific versions of a more generalized `When`. This versatile helper offers an argument to its call back that contains all information about current binding request including the target information. Here is how to register types for a `Data Migration` application using this helper method:

```
Bind<IShippersRepository>().To<ShippersSqlRepository>()
.When(r => r.Target.Name.StartsWith("source"));
Bind<IShippersRepository>().To<ShippersXmlRepository>()
.When(r => r.Target.Name.StartsWith("target"));
```

The preceding code binds `IShippersRepository` to `ShippersSqlRepository` provided that the target parameter name starts with `source`. Similar rule is applied to the second binding as well.

Custom providers

Providers are specialized factory classes that Ninject uses in order to instantiate resolved types. Whenever we bind a service type to a component, we are implicitly associating that service type to a provider that can generate instances of that component. This hidden provider is a generic factory, which can create instances of every given type, and is called `StandardProvider`. Although we can often rely on `StandardProvider` without having to bother about what it does behind the scenes, Ninject also allows us to create and register our custom providers just in case we need to customize the activation process as follows:

```
Bind<IService>().ToProvider<MyService>();
public class MyServiceProvider : Provider<MyService>
{
    protected override MyService CreateInstance(IContext context)
    {
        return new MyService();
    }
}
```

Although extending the `Provider<T>` class is the recommended way to create a custom provider, implementing the `IProvider` interface is enough for a class to be accepted by Ninject as a provider:

```
public interface IProvider
{
    Type Type { get; }
    object Create(IContext context);
}
```

Implementing the data access layer of the data migration application demonstrates how to implement and use a custom provider. We need to add a new class library projects to our solution for each of our data access libraries (SQL data access and XML data access).

Let's start with implementing the `ShippersSqlRepository` class:

```
public class ShippersSqlRepository : IShippersRepository
{
    private readonly NorthwindContext objectContext;
    public ShippersSqlRepository(string northwindConnectionString)
    {
        objectContext =
            new NorthwindContext(northwindConnectionString);
    }

    public IEnumerable<Business.Model.Shipper> GetShippers()
    {  ...  }
    public void AddShipper(Business.Model.Shipper shipper)
    {  ...  }
}
```

Our `ShippersSqlRepository` class needs to be passed a connection string which we will deal with later in this section. We have a similar scenario in the `ShippersXmlRepository` class:

```
public class ShippersXmlRepository : IShippersRepository
{
    private readonly string documentPath;
    public ShippersXmlRepository(string xmlRepositoryPath)
    {
        this.documentPath = xmlRepositoryPath;
    }
```

```
public IEnumerable<Shipper> GetShippers()
{  ...  }

public void AddShipper(Shipper shipper)
{  ...  }
}
```

In this case, we need to pass a file path for the XML data file. These parameters prevent Ninject from instantiating our repositories, because the kernel doesn't have any idea how to resolve the string parameters. So, the following lines are not enough for registering our repositories:

```
Bind<IShippersRepository>().To<ShippersSqlRepository>()
    .When(r => r.Target.Name.StartsWith("source"));
Bind<IShippersRepository>().To<ShippersXmlRepository>()
    .When(r => r.Target.Name.StartsWith("target"));
```

One way of providing the required arguments is using the `WithConstructorArgument` method:

```
connection = ConfigurationManager.AppSettings["northwindConnectionStr
ing"];

Bind<IShippersRepository>()
.To<ShippersSqlRepository>()
.When(r => r.Target.Name.StartsWith("source"))
.WithConstructorArgument("NorthwindConnectionString", connection);

path = ConfigurationManager.ConnectionStrings["xmlRepositoryPath"];

Bind<IShippersRepository>()
.To<ShippersXmlRepository>()
.When(r => r.Target.Name.StartsWith("target"))
.WithConstructorArgument("XmlRepositoryPath",path);
```

It looks good when we don't have to register many repositories which need such configuration. However, in more complicated cases, we need to automate injection of these arguments somehow. This is where a `Provider` class can offer a better solution. All of the settings here are instances of `string`. So, we can create a provider for the `string` type to generate our configuration strings based on the name of the parameter. The provider will look up the parameter name as a configuration key in the application configuration file (either `web.config` or `app.config`), and if such a configuration is defined (as in the following code), it returns its value:

```
public class ConfigurationProvider : Provider<string>
{
    protected override string CreateInstance(IContext context)
    {
        if (context.Request.Target == null)
            throw new Exception("Target required.");
        var paramName = context.Request.Target.Name;
        string value = ConfigurationManager.AppSettings[paramName];
        if (string.IsNullOrEmpty(value))
            value = ConfigurationManager
                    .ConnectionStrings[paramName].ConnectionString;
        return value;
    }
}
```

ConfigurationProvider is given a context object which contains all of the information about the current activation process, including the request object that we mentioned earlier in this chapter. The Request object has information about the target, which in this case is the constructor parameter into which a string instance should be injected. The Target object will be null if this string type is being requested directly from the kernel by using the Get<string>() method. Because we need name of the parameter as the configuration key, we check the target first. Using the target's name, we can look up AppSettings, and in case of we do not find such a setting, we will search in the ConnectionStrings section. Finally, the retrieved value will be returned.

The only problem is that this provider will be registered for the string type and it will affect any string which is going to be resolved by Ninject. In order to specify the strings which are going to be considered as application configurations, we will define a custom attribute and apply it to those parameters as follows:

```
[AttributeUsage(AttributeTargets.Property | AttributeTargets.
Parameter)]
public class ConfigurationAttribute : Attribute { }
```

We have declared that the attribute should only be applied to properties and parameters. Here is how this attribute is applied to the constructor parameter of our repository classes:

```
public ShippersXmlRepository([Configuration]string xmlRepositoryPath)
{
    this.documentPath = xmlRepositoryPath;
}
public ShippersSqlRepository([Configuration]string
northwindConnectionString)
{
```

```
        objectContext = new NorthwindContext(northwindConnectionString);
    }
```

And finally, the binding code is as follows:

```
    Bind<string>().ToProvider<ConfigurationProvider>()
        .WhenTargetHas<ConfigurationAttribute>();
```

Activation context

While overriding the `CreateInstance` method in our provider, we used the context object, which was passed through method parameter. This object, which is represented by the `IContext` interface, contains pretty much of all the information related to the current activation process. Using this object, we can have access to the current binding object, the type being resolved, the type being injected, where in the dependency graph we are, who has requested this resolution, and so on. While resolving a dependency graph, a context object is created for each type being resolved, and this leads to an activation context graph. Starting from each context object, we can also navigate through its parent context nodes until reaching the root of the graph where the initial request is made. When using Ninject, this context object is available wherever we need to make a decision about how to resolve dependencies.

Factory Methods

Factory Methods are another way of informing Ninject how to resolve a dependency. Like creating a provider, we have access to the activation context object to help us make decisions on how to resolve the requested type. However, we don't need to create a new class, and we can just write our resolution logic inline. A Factory Method is a good substitute for a Provider class, where the resolution logic is simple and short. A good example of using a Factory Method is to initialize a logger object in a class. The following is the code to initialize a logger without DI:

```
class ConsumerClass
{
    private ILog log = LogManager.GetLogger(typeof(ConsumerClass));
}
```

We can implement DI in the preceding class using the following code:

```
class ConsumerClass
{
    private ILog log;
    public ConsumerClass(ILog log)
    {
```

```
    // The following line should change
        ICircle circle = new Circle();
        canvas.AddShape(circle);
    }
    for (int i = 0; i < squares; i++)
    {
    // The following line should change
        ISquare square = new Square();
        canvas.AddShape(square);
    }
}
```

The traditional way was to create new instances of the Circle and Square classes directly in the AddShapes method. However, this way we will tightly couple the ShapeService class to the concrete Circle and Square types that is in contrast with DI principles. On the other hand, introducing these dependencies as parameters doesn't meet our requirement, because only one instance per shape will be injected, which will not be enough. In order to solve this problem, we should first create a simple factory interface as follows:

```
public interface IShapeFactory
{
    ICircle CreateCircle();
    ISquare CreateSquare();
}
```

Then, we can introduce this factory interface as the dependency of our ShapeService class:

```
public ShapeService(IShapeFactory factory)
{
    this.factory = factory;
}

public void AddShapes(int circles, int squares, ICanvas canvas)
{
    for (int i = 0; i < circles; i++)
    {
        ICircle circle = factory.CreateCircle();
        canvas.AddShape(circle);
    }
    for (int i = 0; i < squares; i++)
    {
        ISquare square = factory.CreateSquare();
        canvas.AddShape(square);
    }
}
```

The good news is that we don't need to worry about how to implement `IShapeFactory`. Ninject can implement it dynamically and inject the implemented factory into the `ShapeService` class. We just need to add the following code to our type registration segment:

```
Bind<IShapeFactory>().ToFactory();
Bind<ISquare>().To<>(Square);
Bind<ICircle>().To<>(Circle);
```

In order to make use of Ninject factory, we need to add a reference to the `Ninject.Extensions.Factory` library. This either can be added via NuGet or download it from the Ninject official website.

Keep in mind that a factory can have as many methods as required and each method can return any desired type. The methods can have any arbitrary name and have any number of parameters. The only constraint is that the name and type of parameters must conform to the name and type of the constructor parameters of the concrete class, but their order does not matter. Even the number of parameters doesn't need to match and Ninject will try to resolve those parameters which are not provided via the factory interface.

So, if the concrete `Square` class is as follows:

```
public class Square
{
    public Square(Point startPoint, Point endPoint)
    {          ...      }
}
```

The `IShapeFactory` factory interface should look as follows:

```
public interface IShapeFactory
{
    ICircle CreateCircle();
    ISquare CreateSquare(Point startPoint, Point endPoint);
}
```

Alternatively, the `CreateSquare` method could look as follows:

```
ISquare CreateSquare(Point endPoint, Point startPoint);
```

This is the default behaviour of Ninject dynamic factories. However, this default behavior can be overridden by creating customized Instance Providers, which we will learn later in this chapter.

Using convention

Registering convention-based binding for dynamic factories or other on-the-fly implementation generators is slightly different from the regular convention. The difference is that once we have selected assemblies, we should select service types instead of components and then bind them to factory or a custom generator. The following sections describe how to implement these two steps.

Selecting service types

Select an abstraction using any of the following methods:

- `SelectAllIncludingAbstractClasses()`: This method selects all classes including the abstract ones.

- `SelectAllAbstractClasses()`: This method selects just abstract classes.

- `SelectAllInterfaces()`: This method selects all interfaces.

- `SelectAllTypes()`: This method selects all types (`classes`, `interfaces`, `structs`, `enums`, and primitive types).

The following code binds all interfaces within the selected assembly to dynamic factories:

```
kernel.Bind(x => x
    .FromAssembliesMatching("factories")
    .SelectAllInterfaces()
    .BindToFactory());
```

Defining Binding Generator

Use one of the following methods to define appropriate binding generator:

- `BindToFactory`: This method registers the projected types as dynamic factories.

- `BindWith`: This method creates a binding using a binding generator argument. Creating a binding generator is just a matter of implementing the `IBindingGenerator` interface.

The following example binds all of those interfaces of the current assembly whose names end with `Factory` to dynamic factories.

```
kernel.Bind(x => x
    .FromThisAssembly()
    .SelectAllInterfaces()
    .EndingWith("Factory")
    .BindToFactory());
```

Telecom Switch example

In the following example, we will write a service for a Telecom center that returns the current status of a given telecom switch. Telecom switches which are manufactured by different vendors may offer different ways to be queried. Some of them support communication via TCP/IP protocol and some of them simply write their status in a file.

Let's start by creating the `Switch` class as follows:

```
public class Switch
{
    public string Name { get; set; }
    public string Vendor { get; set; }
    public bool SupportsTcpIp { get; set; }
}
```

To collect the status of a switch we create an interface as follows:

```
public interface IStatusCollector
{
    string GetStatus(Switch @switch);
}
```

 In C#, the @ symbol allows us to use a reserved word as a variable name.

We need two different implementations of this interface for two different switch types; the switches which support TCP/IP communication and those that don't. Let's name them as `TcpStatusCollector` and `FileStatusCollector` respectively. We also need to declare a factory interface which can create instances of these two concrete `StatusCollectors`:

```
public interface IStatusCollectorFactory
{
    IStatusCollector GetTcpStatusCollector();
    IStatusCollector GetFileStatusCollector();
}
```

And finally it comes to the `SwitchService` class:

```
public class SwitchService
{
    private readonly IStatusCollectorFactory factory;
    public SwitchService(IStatusCollectorFactory factory)
    {
        this.factory = factory;
    }

    public string GetStatus(Switch @switch)
    {
        IStatusCollector collector;
        if (@switch.SupportsTcpIp)
            collector = factory.GetTcpStatusCollector();
        else
            collector = factory.GetFileStatusCollector();
        return collector.GetStatus(@switch);
    }
}
```

The `SwitchService` class will never create an instance of `FileStatusCollector` if all of the given switches support TCP/IP. This way, the `SwitchService` class is only injected with the dependencies that it really needs rather than all of the types for which there is a possibility of need.

`IStatusCollectorFactory` has two factory methods both of which are of the same type. Now, how does Ninject's implementation of this factory understand how to resolve `IStatusCollector`? The magic lies in the name of the factory methods. Whenever the name of a factory method starts with `Get`, it indicates that the type will be resolved using named binding, where the name is the rest of the method name. For example if the name of the factory's method is `GetXXX`, the factory will try to find a binding named `XXX`. So, the type registration section for this example should be as follows:

```
Kernel.Bind(x => x.FromThisAssembly()
                  .SelectAllInterfaces()
                  .EndingWith("Factory")
                  .BindToFactory());
```

```
Kernel.Bind(x => x.FromThisAssembly()
                .SelectAllClasses()
                .InheritedFrom<IStatusCollector>()
                .BindAllInterfaces()
                .Configure((b, comp) => b.Named(comp.Name)));
```

The first convention binds all of the interfaces whose names end with `Factory` to `Factory` and the second one registers named binding for all implementations of `IStatusCollector` in such a way that each binding is named after its component's name. It is equivalent to the following single bindings:

```
Bind<IStatusCollector>().To<TcpStatusCollector>()
    .Named("TcpStatusCollector");
Bind<IStatusCollector>().To<FileStatusCollector>()
    .Named("FileStatusCollector");
```

However, using single binding in this relies on `string` names, which is error prone and the relation can easily break by a typo. There is another way of naming for single bindings which is only available while referencing `Ninject.Extensions.Factory` and is especially designed for such scenarios. We can use the `NamedLikeFactoryMethod` helper method instead of the `Named` helper to name a binding for a factory:

```
Bind<IStatusCollector>().To<FileStatusCollector>()
.NamedLikeFactoryMethod(
    (IStatusCollectorFactory f) => f.GetFileStatusCollector());
```

It means that we are defining a named binding with the name that the indicated factory method suggests.

Please note that using conventions is always the preferred approach.

Custom Instance Providers

A dynamic factory doesn't instantiate requested types directly. Instead, it uses another object named Instance Provider (don't get confused with Provider) to create an instance of a type. The Instance Provider is given some information about the factory's method including the name of the method, its return type, and its parameters based on which the Instance Provider should resolve the requested object. As long as a factory is not assigned a custom Instance Provider, it uses its default Instance Provider, which is named `StandardInstanceProvider`. We can assign a custom Instance Provider to a factory while registering it as follows:

```
Kernel.Bind(x => x.FromThisAssembly()
                    .SelectAllInterfaces()
                    .EndingWith("Factory")
                    .BindToFactory(() => new MyInstanceProvider()));
```

In order for Ninject to accept a class as an Instance Provider, it is enough for the class to implement the `IInstanceProvider` interface. However, the easier way is to inherit from `StandardInstanceProvider` and override the desired members.

The following code shows how to define an Instance Provider which gets the name of the binding from `NamedAttribute` rather than the method name:

```
class NameAttributeInstanceProvider : StandardInstanceProvider
{
    protected override string GetName(System.Reflection.MethodInfo
methodInfo, object[] arguments)
    {
        var nameAttribute = methodInfo
            .GetCustomAttributes(typeof(NamedAttribute), true)
            .FirstOrDefault() as NamedAttribute;
        if (nameAttribute != null)
            return nameAttribute.Name;
        return base.GetName(methodInfo, arguments);
    }
}
```

Using this custom Instance Provider, we can choose any desired name for our factory methods and then use an attribute to specify the required binding name. Since the Ninject `NamedAttribute` attribute doesn't apply to methods, we will create our own attribute as follows:

```
public class BindingNameAttribute:Attribute
{
    public BindingNameAttribute(string name)
    {
        this.Name = name;
    }
    public string Name { get; set; }
}
```

The factory interface can now be defined as follows:

```
public interface IStatusCollectorFactory
{
    [BindingName("TcpStatusCollector"")]"
    IStatusCollector GreateTcpStatusCollector();

    [BindingName("FileStatusCollector"")]"
    IStatusCollector GreateFileStatusCollector();
}
```

And the factory type registration should be as follows:

```
Bind<IStatusCollectorFactory>()
    .ToFactory(() = > new NameAttributeInstanceProvider());
```

Func

Another way of creating multiple instances of a dependency in a consumer class is by using the Func delegate. Whenever Ninject detects Func<IService> rather than IService itself, it injects a factory method which can create an implementation of IService. It is not as powerful as the factory interface, but it is easier to use because there is no need to define an interface:

```
public class Consumer
{
    private readonly Func<IService> factory;
    public Consumer(Func<IService> factory)
    {
        this.factory = factory;
    }
    public void Consume()
    {
        // A new instance of service will be created each time
        // the following factory method is called
        var service = this.factory();
        ...
    }
}
```

Func also supports passing parameters, but since it doesn't provide any information about the arguments, using Func in such scenarios is not recommended.

Lazy

As soon as a consumer class is being created, all of its dependencies are instantiated and injected, even though they are not being used at that very moment. This can slow down the instantiation of the consumer class especially when the dependencies are expensive. For instance, a dependency which needs network communication while being created can also slow down the activation of its consumer class. Using `Lazy<IService>` instead of `IService`, defers the instantiation of the dependency to the time when it is requested:

```
public class Consumer
{
    private readonly Lazy<IService> lazyService;
    public Cunsumer(Lazy<IService> service)
    {
        this.lazyService = service;
    }

    public void Consume()
    {
     // service will be created once the Value requested.
        var service = lazyService.Value;
        ...
    }
}
```

Ninject automatically creates and injects a `Lazy` object, and there is no need to register a separate binding for it.

Summary

We studied the most common DI patterns and antipatterns related to Ninject. Multibinding means binding a single service type to multiple concrete types and has two scenarios of the Plugin model and contextual binding. Providers are a kind of factories that are specialized for Ninject to be used for creating new instances of resolved types. We can create our own providers by deriving from the `Provider<T>` class. A `Factory` method is a substitute for `Provider`, where the activation logic is short and simple and instantiation of the service type is not as simple as calling the constructor of the implementation. Introducing a dependency as `Lazy<dependency>` informs Ninject to defer instantiation of that dependency whenever that dependency is requested.

4
Ninject in Action

This chapter shows how to set up different types of applications using Ninject. We will implement a concrete scenario using a variety of application types to see how to set up and use Ninject for injecting the dependencies. By the end of this chapter, the user will be able to set up and use Ninject for all kinds of described applications.

Topics covered:

- Windows Forms applications
- WPF and Silverlight applications
- ASP.NET MVC applications
- WCF applications
- ASP.NET Web Forms applications

Although how Ninject helps us inject dependencies into our application components is the same across different types of applications, setting these applications up varies according to their architectures. Some new frameworks such as ASP .NET MVC are intentionally designed to support DI, while some older frameworks such as ASP .NET are not even capable of supporting all DI patterns.

We have already learned most of the features that Ninject offers and this chapter helps us to put them together in a project. We will implement several applications, each of which includes a data access layer, a domain layer, and a presentation layer. The first two layers will be shared among all of them and also will be used in combination with a service layer to implement a WCF service application.

Our objective is to perform Create and Read operations out of **CRUD (Create, Read, Update, and Delete)** operations across the `Customers` table of the `Northwind` database, which is the sample database for all editions of Microsoft SQL Server, and should already exist on your machine if you have any version of SQL Server installed. Although we will implement a SQL data access as our data access layer, the entire application is independent from a concrete data access, and uses an abstraction as its repository; but our Model conforms to the `Customers` table with selective fields.

The source code of this sample is available for download on the publisher's website.

Let's start with the domain layer, which will be shared among all of the applications that we will create. Create a new class library in Visual Studio and name it `Northwind.Core`. It will contain our domain models and logic. Add a new class and name it `Customer`. To keep things simple, we select only a few fields of the `Northwind Customer` entity. So, create a class that has string properties for `ID`, `CompanyName`, `City`, `PostalCode`, and `Phone`.

Then, we will define the abstraction of our `Customer` repository. For this sample project, we only define those operations that we need (create and read), but we can add other operations to it later. Create the following interface in `Northwind.Core`:

```
public interface ICustomerRepository
{
    IEnumerable<Customer> GetAll();
    Customer Get(string customerID);
    void Add(Customer customer);
}
```

The rest of the application will use this interface as the repository abstraction for the `Customer` entity.

Now, add another class library project and name it `Northwind.SqlDataAccess`. As far as we implement `ICustomerRepository`, it doesn't matter to the rest of the application how the data access is implemented. We use **Entity Framework** as our data access solution. So, let's add a new **ADO.NET Entity Data Model** to the project, and name it `NorthwindModel`. For this sample, we only need the `Customers` table. We can also remove the fields of this table that we don't need. `Customer_ID`, `Company_Name`, `City`, `Postal_Code`, and `Phone` are all of the fields that we need.

Then add a class named `SqlCustomerRepository` which should implement
`ICustomerRepository`:

```
public class SqlCustomerRepository : ICustomerRepository
{
    // The Mapper will be discussed in a moment
    private readonly Mapper mapper;
    private readonly NorthwindEntities context;

    public void Add(Core.Customer domainCustomer)
    {    }

    IEnumerable<Core.Customer> ICustomerRepository.GetAll()
    {    }

    public Core.Customer Get(string customerID)
    {    }
}
```

The following is the implementation of the `Add` method:

```
public void Add(Core.Customer domainCustomer)
{
    // Converts domainCustomer to customer
    var customer = mapper.Map(domainCustomer);
    context.Customers.AddObject(customer);
    context.SaveChanges();
}
```

Please note that the type of the `Customer` entity generated by Entity Framework is
different from our domain model `Customer`. Thus, we need a **mapper** to convert
these two types to each other. We have had two dependencies for this class so far:
a mapper and the entity container context. Let's see how we should declare the
constructor of the `SqlCustomerRepository` class:

```
public SqlCustomerRepository(Mapper mapper, NorthwindEntities context)
{
    this.mapper = mapper;
    this.context = context;
}
```

The next step is to add the Read methods:

```
IEnumerable<Core.Customer> ICustomerRepository.GetAll()
{
    return mapper.Map(context.Customers);
}


public Core.Customer Get(string customerID)
{
    var customer = context.Customers
        .SingleOrDefault(c => c.Customer_ID == customerID);

    return mapper.Map(customer);
}
```

Again, we use the mapper to convert the auto generated Customer entity to our
domain Customer mode.

 There are third-party libraries that automate the mapping logic.
AutoMapper and ValueInjecter are two examples.

The following is our implementation of the Mapper class:

```
public class Mapper
{
    public Core.Customer Map(Customer customer)
    {
        if (customer == null)
        {
            return null;
        }
        return new Core.Customer
                {
                    ID = customer.Customer_ID,
                    City = customer.City,
                    CompanyName = customer.Company_Name,
                    Phone = customer.Phone,
                    PostalCode = customer.Postal_Code
                };
    }

    public Customer Map(Core.Customer customer)
    {
        if (customer==null)
```

```
    {
        return null;
    }
    return new Customer
    {
        Customer_ID = customer.ID,
        City = customer.City,
        Company_Name = customer.CompanyName,
        Phone = customer.Phone,
        Postal_Code = customer.PostalCode
    };
}

public IEnumerable<Core.Customer> Map(IEnumerable<Customer>
customers)
{
    return customers.Select(Map);
}
}
```

The logic of the `Mapper` class is pretty simple. It maps null objects to `null` and non-null objects to their corresponding entity. Note that in the last `Map` method, the LINQ `Select` method is using the first `Map` method as a *method group*, and we don't need to use a lambda expression to call it. It is equivalent to the following expression:

```
return customers.Select(c => Map(c));
```

Having prepared our domain and data access layers, we are now ready to move ahead to implement our first presentation scenario, which is a Windows Forms application.

Windows Forms applications

Windows Forms is one of the most straightforward application types to implement DI. Just like Console application, it does not need special Ninject configuration. The `Main` method in the `Program` class is where we can use as a Composition Root (refer to *Dependency Injection In .NET* by *Mark Seemann*, published by *Manning Publication Co.*), and the framework components such as Form classes do not require to have a parameterless constructor, which makes implementation of constructor injection easily possible.

Add a new Windows Forms application to the `Northwind` solution, and name it `Northwind.Winforms`.

Add references to the `Northwind.Core` project, `Ninject.Extensions.Conventions` and `Ninject.Extensions.Factory`. Note that the extensions implicitly add a reference to `Ninject` if you are using NuGet. Otherwise, you need to add it manually.

We continue with the `MainForm`, which is going to have a `DataGrid` to show the list of customers.

Add a `DataGrid` and bind it to a `BindingSource` control. You can also add the `Customer` class as a data source to the project. In the source code of the `MainForm`, either override the `OnLoad` method or add a handler for `Load` event:

```
protected override void OnLoad(EventArgs e)
{
    base.OnLoad(e);
    LoadCustomers();
}

private void LoadCustomers()
{
    customerBindingSource.DataSource = repository.GetAll();
}
```

We introduced the `LoadCustomers` method to populate customers, because we will need to call it again later in this form. In this method, we need an instance of our `Customer` repository. This introduces the first dependency of the `MainForm`:

```
private readonly ICustomerRepository repository;
public MainForm(ICustomerRepository repository)
{
    this.repository = repository;
    InitializeComponent();
}
```

Then, we need to add another Form for creating a new customer. Let's call it `CustomerForm`.

We need to have a `BindingSource` bound to the `Customer` project data source. The `Text` property of all `TextBox` controls should be bound to their corresponding fields of the `Customer` model. The easiest way is to drag the data source and drop it into the form in details mode.

The following code shows the code behind of `CustomerForm`:

```
public partial class CustomerForm : Form
{
    private readonly ICustomerRepository repository;
    public CustomerForm(ICustomerRepository repository)
    {
        this.repository = repository;
        InitializeComponent();
        customerBindingSource.Add(new Customer());
    }

    private void saveButton_Click(object sender, EventArgs e)
    {
        customerBindingSource.EndEdit();
        var customer = customerBindingSource.Current as Customer;
        repository.Add(customer);
    }
}
```

`ICustomerRepository` is the only dependency of this class, which is introduced in the constructor and will be injected later. Note that the `Customer` object is created using its constructor rather than injected. The reason is that `Customer` is an entity, and entities should not be created by an `IoC` container. It is also the same for a **Data Transfer Object (DTO)**.

Now that we are done with `CustomerForm`, we need to show it from `MainForm` in the `Click` event handler of `saveButton`. An instance of `CustomerForm` should *not* be achieved in any of the following ways:

- Calling `new CustomerForm()` because this way we will have to resolve its dependencies ourselves rather than Ninject

- Calling `kernel.Get<CustomerForm>()` because we will need to make our class dependent on `Kernel`

- Introducing a new dependency to `CustomerForm` in constructor, because this way we will receive only one instance of `CustomerForm`, while after closing that instance, we will need another one for subsequent clicks on the **Save** button

So what are we going to do? Here is where the factories come into play. Thanks to a Ninject built-in `Factory` feature, we simply need to declare the following interface:

```
public interface IFormFactory
{
    T Create<T>() where T : Form;
}
```

If we need to provide more arguments than those Ninject can resolve to the requested form, we can add more overloads for the previous generic `Create` method to our factory providing those parameters:

```
private void saveButton_Click(object sender, EventArgs e)
{
    var customerForm = formFactory.Create<CustomerForm>();
    if (customerForm.ShowDialog(this) == DialogResult.OK)
    {
        LoadCustomers();
    }
}
```

This introduces the second dependency of `MainForm`:

```
private readonly ICustomerRepository repository;
private readonly IFormFactory formFactory;

public MainForm(ICustomerRepository repository, IFormFactory
formFactory)
{
    this.repository = repository;
    this.formFactory = formFactory;
    InitializeComponent();
}
```

The next step is to define our service registrations. The Composition Root for a Windows Forms application is the `Main` method in the `Program` class. So, add the following lines to the `Main` method:

```
using (var kernel = new StandardKernel())
{
    kernel.Bind(x => x.FromAssembliesMatching("Northwind.*")
                      .SelectAllClasses()
                      .BindAllInterfaces());

    kernel.Bind(x => x.FromThisAssembly()
                      .SelectAllInterfaces()
```

```
                    .EndingWith("Factory")
                    .BindToFactory()
                    .Configure(c => c.InSingletonScope())));

    var mainForm = kernel.Get<MainForm>();
    Application.Run(mainForm);
}
```

The first convention rule selects all of the assemblies starting with "Northwind" and binds their types to their base interfaces. This way, we are avoiding unwanted or possibly duplicated bindings for other assemblies, for example, Ninject assemblies.

The second rule registers the interfaces whose names end with "Factory" as Singleton factories.

WPF and Silverlight applications

Although Silverlight is a lighter version of **Windows Presentation Foundation (WPF)**, these two frameworks are so similar that they can be treated the same way in terms of DI. Both frameworks offer a single startup location for the application in their App.xaml file, which can be used as the Composition Root. The view engine for both frameworks is based on **Extensible Application Markup Language (XAML)** and they both support **Model-View-ViewModel (MVVM)** architecture.

In this section we will implement the Northwind scenario using MVVM pattern which can be applied to either WPF or a Silverlight application. In MVVM, the application consists of the following key parts:

- **Model**: The domain Models that represent business entities, and we have already created them in our domain layer.

- **View**: A XAML UI file which is usually a Window or a User Control with minimal or no code behind.

- **ViewModel**: As the name suggests, it is a Model for the View. It contains the presentation logic and exposes the application outputs from Models to the View or gets inputs from the View via property binding.

In this application, we are going to have a `MainView` to populate the list of customers and a `CustomerView` which will be shown when the **Save** button on `MainView` is clicked. The Views look like those we created for our Windows Forms application in the previous section. Each View is going to have a View Model, which will be assigned to its `DataContext` property. *Figure 4.1* shows the relation between our Views and their corresponding ViewModels:

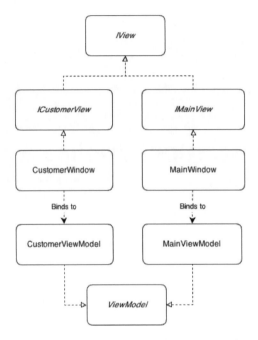

Figure 4.1: The relation between our Views and their corresponding ViewModels

Let's start by implementing `MainViewModel`. In MVVM, the ViewModels are totally independent from their Views. Any data which is going to be presented in the View should be exposed as a property. The following property exposes the list of customers:

```
public IEnumerable<Customer> Customers
{
    get { return repository.GetAll(); }
}
```

This property suggests that the first dependency of the `MainViewModel` class should be our repository. As soon as we get to know our dependencies, we should declare them, as shown in the following code:

```
private readonly ICustomerRepository repository;
```

```
public MainViewModel(ICustomerRepository repository)
{
    this.repository = repository;
}
```

The `MainWindow` will then have a `DataGrid` control or any other proper control to present the data exposed by this property:

```
<DataGrid IsReadOnly="True" ItemsSource="{Binding Customers}" />
```

Now we create the `CustomerViewModel` class which is responsible for adding new customers to the repository, as shown in the following snippet. It exposes a single `Customer` Model via a property which can later be modified using a View.

```
public Customer Customer
{
    get
    {
        return customer;
    }
}
```

The `customer` field is instantiated with a `Customer` object in constructor. The following XAML code shows how the `CustomerWindow` controls are bound to the properties of the `Customer` object, which is exposed by the `Customer` property:

```
<StackPanel DataContext="{Binding Customer}">
    <Label >Customer ID</Label>
    <TextBox Text="{Binding ID}"/>
    <Label>Company Name</Label>
    <TextBox Text="{Binding CompanyName}"/>
    <Label >City</Label>
    <TextBox Text="{Binding City}"/>
    <Label>Postal Code</Label>
    <TextBox Text="{Binding PostalCode}"/>
    <Label>Phone</Label>
    <TextBox Text="{Binding Phone}"/>
</StackPanel>
```

The next step is to add the modified customer to the repository and close the `CustomerWindow` as soon as the user clicks on the **Save** button. A ViewModel is not supposed to see its View and instead, the View observes its ViewModel to change any UI state. Hence, in order to close the `CustomerWindow`, we cannot call its `Close` method, because we have no reference to the View.

Instead, we can have a `DialogResult` property in the ViewModel which can be set to notify the View to be closed:

```
public void Save(object paramer)
{
    repository.Add(Customer);
    DialogResult = true;
}

public bool? DialogResult
{
    get
    {
        return dialogResult;
    }
    set
    {
        dialogResult = value;
        OnPropertyChanged("DialogResult");
    }
}
```

The `OnPropertyChanged` method is implemented in the abstract `ViewModel` class which is inherited by `CustomerViewModel`. It is used to notify the View about the changes of a property, so that View reacts to those changes.

The `DialogResult` property of a Window is not a *Dependency Property* and hence, cannot accept a binding. To work around this problem, we can create a `WindowHelper` class which offers a `DialogResult` *Attached Property*, and can be attached to a Window like the following:

```
<Window x:Class="Northwind.Wpf.Views.CustomerWindow"
xmlns="http://schemas.microsoft.com/winfx/2006/xaml/presentation"
xmlns:x="http://schemas.microsoft.com/winfx/2006/xaml"
xmlns:Infrastructure="clr-namespace:Northwind.Wpf.Infrastructure"
Infrastructure:WindowHelper.DialogResult=»{Binding DialogResult}»>
```

Note that a Window's `DialogResult` property is assignable only when the Window is shown as a dialog using its `ShowDialog` method. In normal circumstances, you can set the `IsClosed` attached property of `WindowHelper` which calls the `Close` method of Window rather than setting its `DialogResult` property, as shown in the following code.

Dependency properties, Attached properties, and how to implement a
`WindowHelper` is beyond the scope of this book; however, you can view the details in
the downloaded samples of this book.

```
public static readonly DependencyProperty DialogResultProperty =
    DependencyProperty.RegisterAttached(
    "DialogResult", typeof(bool?), typeof(WindowHelper),
    new UIPropertyMetadata(null, OnPropertyChanged));

private static void OnPropertyChanged(DependencyObject d,
DependencyPropertyChangedEventArgs e)
{
    var view = d as IView;
    if (view == null)
    {
        throw new NotSupportedException("Only IView type is
supported.");
    }
    view.DialogResult = (bool?)e.NewValue;
}
```

Now we need to call the `Save` method when the user clicks the **Save** button.
In MVVM, we use commands to let a View call ViewModel's methods.
The following is the `SaveCommand` property in `CustomerViewModel` to be
exposed to the `CustomerWindow`:

```
public ICommand SaveCommand
{
    get
    {
        return saveCommand;
    }
}
```

The following XAML code shows the **Save** button, which is bound to the
`SaveCommand`:

```
<Button Command="{Binding SaveCommand}" >Save</Button>
```

We have used `ICommand` which is an interface of the .NET Framework, and is recognized by WPF components. Now we should implement `ICommand`. In order to make our concrete command independent from our domain logic, we use an `ActionCommand`, which is a simple version of the `RelayCommand` pattern:

```
public class ActionCommand : ICommand
{
    private readonly Action<object> action;
    private readonly Func<object, bool> canExecute = p => true;

    public ActionCommand(Action<object> action,
                         Func<object, bool> canExecute = null)
    {
        if (action == null)
        {
            throw new ArgumentNullException("action");
        }
        this.action = action;

        if (canExecute != null)
        {
            this.canExecute = canExecute;
        }
    }

    public void Execute(object parameter)
    {
        action(parameter);
    }

    public bool CanExecute(object parameter)
    {
        return canExecute(parameter);
    }

    public event EventHandler CanExecuteChanged;
}
```

In order to create an instance of `ActionCommand` and assign it to the `SaveCommand`, we need an abstract factory. Ninject can create this factory on the fly if we define its interface:

```
public interface ICommandFactory
{
    ICommand CreateCommand(Action<object> action,
```

```
                    Func<object, bool> canExecute = null);
}
```

Using this factory in a ViewModel class, we can create as many Command objects as
we need. Now that we have identified the dependencies of CustomerViewModel, let's
have a look at its constructor:

```
public CustomerViewModel(ICustomerRepository repository,
                         ICommandFactory commandFactory)
{
    this.repository = repository;
    this.saveCommand = commandFactory.CreateCommand(Save);
    this.customer = new Customer();
}
```

Now that we have created CustomerViewModel, we can go back to the MainViewModel
class and implement the logic of showing the CustomerWindow method:

```
private void CreateCustomer(object param)
{
    var customerView = viewFactory.CreateView<ICustomerView>();
    if (customerView.ShowDialog() == true)
    {
        // Refresh the list
        OnPropertyChanged("Customers");
    }
}
```

The MainViewModel doesn't have any idea about CustomerWindow and it doesn't
need to. It just interacts with ICustomerView which provides an interface containing
only those methods that a ViewModel may need to call. This interface can then be
implemented with any View class. The View does not even have to be an XAML
window. The following code shows the IView interface which is inherited by
ICustomerView:

```
public interface IView
{
    bool? ShowDialog();
    void Show();
    void Close();
    bool? DialogResult { get; set; }
}
```

The `MainViewModel` doesn't even care how the concrete `Customer` View will implement `Show` or `Close`. It may be a `TabPage` in a `TabControl`, a simulated popup, or a *Mock* object.

In order to create an instance of the concrete View, we need a view factory:

```
public interface IViewFactory
{
    T CreateView<T>() where T : IView;
    T CreateView<T>(ViewModel viewModel) where T : IView;
}
```

The constructor of `MainViewModel` introduces all of its three dependencies as the following code shows:

```
public MainViewModel(ICustomerRepository repository,
                     IViewFactory viewFactory,
                     ICommandFactory commandFactory)
{
    this.repository = repository;
    this.viewFactory = viewFactory;
    createCustomerCommand =   commandFactory.
CreateCommand(CreateCustomer);

}
```

Now that we have introduced all of our dependencies, we need to compose the application. The starting point of a WPF and Silverlight application is the `App` class which is defined within the `App.xaml` file. We need to remove the `MainWindow` from `StartupUri` of `App.xaml` and either handle the `Startup` event or override the `OnStartup` method of the `App` class to define the application's composition. It should include the following code block:

```
using (var kernel = new StandardKernel())
{
    kernel.Bind(x => x.FromAssembliesMatching("Northwind.*")
                .SelectAllClasses()
                .BindAllInterfaces());

    kernel.Bind(x => x.FromThisAssembly()
                .SelectAllInterfaces()
                .EndingWith("Factory")
                .BindToFactory()
                .Configure(c=>c.InSingletonScope())));

    var mainWindow = kernel.Get<IMainView>();
    mainWindow.Show();
}
```

The convention rules are the same as our WinForms application and finally the pre-existing code, which shows that the `MainWindow` is replaced with our code which calls the `Show` method of the concrete implementation of `IMainView`.

ASP.NET MVC applications

Using Ninject in Windows client applications (WPF and Windows Forms) was not much different from using it in a Console application. We didn't need any certain configuration to set up Ninject in such applications, because in Windows client applications the developer has the control of instantiating UI components (Forms or Windows), and can easily delegate this control to Ninject. In Web applications, however, it is not the same, because the framework is responsible of instantiating the UI. So, we need to somehow tell the framework to delegate that responsibility to Ninject. Fortunately, asking the ASP.NET .MVC framework to do so is easily possible, but it is not the same for Web Forms applications.

Thanks to Ninject's MVC extension, we don't even need to bother setting up MVC framework to support DI. Instead, Ninject's MVC extension will do it for us. In this section, we will implement the Northwind customers scenario using Ninject in an ASP.NET MVC 3 application. Ninject MVC extension also supports other versions of the MVC framework.

Add a new ASP .NET MVC3 Web application to the Northwind solution with references to the `Northwind.Core` project and Ninject `Conventions` extension.

We should also reference Ninject MVC extension. The easiest way is to install the `Ninject.Mvc3` package using NuGet. Keep in mind that although the name of the package is `Ninject.Mvc3`, it is upward compatible with newer versions of the MVC framework. Alternatively, we could download the `Ninject.Web.Mvc` binary from GitHub and reference it from our project. In this case, we also needed to reference the `Ninject` and `Ninject.Web.Common` libraries. These libraries are referenced automatically if we install the `Ninject.Mvc3` package using NuGet. NuGet also adds the `App_Start` folder containing a file named `NinjectWebCommon.cs` to the project. The `NinjectWebCommon` class contains a `Start()` method that will be the starting point of the application. It sets up everything to hook Ninject to MVC framework. So, once we have installed Ninject MVC extension using NuGet, we do not need to do anything else to set up our application, and everything will be already there for us. This is because NuGet allows packages to add files to the project as a part of their installation process. The `NinjectWebCommon` class has a method named `CreateKernel` which can be used as the Composition Root to register our services. We will talk more about this class in the next section.

If we reference Ninject libraries manually using separately downloaded binary files, we should make the following changes to the MvcApplication class located under the Global.asax file:

1. The MvcApplication class should derive from the NinjectHttpApplication class, rather than System.Web.HttpApplication.

2. Instead of having the Application_Start method as the starting point, we should override the OnApplicationStarted method, and anything within Application_Start should go to OnApplicationStarted.

3. We should override CreateKernel and use it for service registration.

The following code shows the CreateKernel method:

```
protected override IKernel CreateKernel()
{
    var kernel = new StandardKernel();
    kernel.Load(new ServiceRegistration());
    return kernel;
}
```

Even if we use NuGet to set up our project, we can delete the App_Start folder, and use Global.asax as described previously. In this case, we can remove references to the WebActivator and Microsoft.Web.Infrastructure libraries that NuGet has created. It is up to you which approach to use, as they do exactly the same thing in two different ways. The first one is easier to use and does not need any extra efforts to set up the application; while the second one uses the existing Global.asax file as the application startup point and doesn't require additional files or libraries to be referenced. In this example, we use the Global.asax file as starting point. In the next section, we will use the App_Start and NinjectWebCommon classes which NuGet creates.

Let's start implementing the presentation of customers list in our application. Open the HomeController class and add a constructor which introduces our ICustomerRepository interface as its parameter:

```
private readonly ICustomerRepository repository;

public HomeController(ICustomerRepository repository)
{
    this.repository = repository;
}
```

The next step is to modify the `Index` action method as follows:

```
public ActionResult Index()
{
    var customers = repository.GetAll();
    return View(customers);
}
```

It uses the `ICustomerRepository` interface to populate customers. Please note that we don't need to create a new Model for customer, and the one that we have already created in our domain layer is being used here. Then, delete the existing `Index.cshtml` View and add a new one with List scaffold template and our `Customer` domain model as the Model class.

Now, add the `Create` action methods as follows:

```
public ActionResult Create()
{
    return View();
}


[HttpPost]
public ActionResult Create(Customer customer)
{
    if (ModelState.IsValid)
    {
        repository.Add(customer);
        return RedirectToAction("Index");
    }
    return View();
}
```

The first one is called when the hyperlink **Create New** is clicked using HTTP GET method, and the second one is called when the `Create` View is submitted using HTTP POST method. The created customer Model is passed to the `Create` method and can be added to the repository. Checking the `ModelState.IsValid` property is for server-side validation. We can now add a `Create` View for this action with `Core.Customer` as Model class and the Create scaffold template.

Validator injection

Now, we need to add some validation rules to our `Customer` Model class. MVC framework supports different kinds of validation including annotation-based validation in which we use validation attributes on the properties of the Model to define the validation rules:

```
public class Customer
{
    [Required]
    public string ID { get; set; }
    [Required]
    public string CompanyName { get; set; }
    public string City { get; set; }
    public string PostalCode { get; set; }
    [StringLength(10)]
    public string Phone { get; set; }
}
```

The validation attributes are not part of MVC library, and this makes it possible to apply them to our `Customer` Model within our domain layer. This way, we can share these validation rules among other UI frameworks as well. We just need to reference the `System.ComponentModel.DataAnnotations` library in our domain project. MVC framework automatically validates the Model based on the provided attributes. But these attributes are limited to basic validation rules. What if we need to check whether the provided ID for our customer is not duplicated? In such scenarios, we need to create our custom validation attributes:

```
public class UniqueCustomerIdAttribute : ValidationAttribute
{
    [Inject]
    public ICustomerValidator Validator { get; set; }

    public override bool IsValid(object value)
    {
        if (Validator == null)
        {
            throw new Exception("Validator is not specified.");
        }
        if (string.IsNullOrEmpty(value as string))
        {
            return false;
        }
        return Validator.ValidateUniqueness(value as string);
    }
}
```

```
            this.log = log;
    }
}
```

It is not possible to register a type binding for `ILogger` using the `To<T>` method, because the concrete logger has to be created by calling the `LogManager.GetLogger` method rather than the constructor of a concrete logger. In this case, we can use a Factory Method in order to inform Ninject about creating a new instance of the logger:

```
Bind<ILog>().ToMethod(ctx => LogManager.GetLogger(ctx.Request.
ParentRequest.Service));));
```

The type of `ctx` is `IContext` and we are getting type of the `Consumer` class from the `Service` property of the parent request of Ninject Activation Context.

This example was just to demonstrate how to employ a Factory Method, and is not a best practice for logging, because it is requiring the application to have a reference to the logger library. One of the best practices for logging will be discussed in *Chapter 5, Doing More with Extensions*.

Dynamic factories

As long as we know all the dependencies of a class and in scenarios where we only need one instance of them, it is easy to introduce a list of the dependencies in the constructor of the class. But there are cases where we may need to create more instances of a dependency in a class as a single instance that Ninject injects is not enough. There are also cases where we don't know which services a consumer may require, because it may require different services in different circumstances, and it doesn't make sense to instantiate all of them while creating the class. In such scenarios, factories can help. We can design our class so that it depends on a factory, rather than the objects that the factory can create. Then, we can command that factory to create the required services on demand and in any required number.

We will see two examples each of which addresses one of the preceding cases and demonstrates the solution that Ninject offers.

The Shape Factory example

In the first example we will create a Graphic library. It contains a `ShapeService` class, which offers an `AddShapes` method to add a given number of specific `IShape` objects to a given `ICanvas` object:

```
public void AddShapes(int circles, int squares, ICanvas canvas)
{
    for (int i = 0; i < circles; i++)
    {
```

By deriving from `ValidationAttribute` and overriding its `IsValid` method, we can define a custom validation attribute. This validator uses an object of the type `ICustomerValidator` to validate the given value, which is a customer ID across the repository to check whether it is unique or duplicated. The following is the implementation of `ICustomerValidator`:

```
public class CustomerValidator : ICustomerValidator
{
    private readonly ICustomerRepository repository;

    public CustomerValidator(ICustomerRepository repository)
    {
        this.repository = repository;
    }

    public bool ValidateUniqueness(string customerID)
    {
        return repository.Get(customerID) == null;
    }
}
```

Validation is successful, provided the repository cannot find any existing customer with the given customer ID.

You may have noticed that in the `UniqueCustomerIdAttribute` class, we didn't introduce the `ICustomerValidator` interface as a dependency in the constructor. The reason is that it is not possible to apply an attribute which requires constructor parameters without providing its arguments. That's why we used the Property Injection pattern, rather than Constructor Injection. Although this attribute should be instantiated by MVC framework, Ninject can inject the dependency before the `IsValid` method is called. Now, you may be wondering that applying the `[Inject]` attribute in our domain layer will make it dependent on Ninject. Well, it didn't, because we didn't use the Ninject version of the `[Inject]` attribute. Instead, we created another `InjectAttribute` class in our `Core` library. We discussed about how to set up Ninject to use another attribute instead of its internal `[Inject]` attribute in *Chapter 3, Meeting real-world Requirements*. This way, we don't have to have a reference to the Ninject library, and can even replace Ninject with other DI containers without needing to touch the domain layer.

We can now add the `UniqueCustomerIdAttribute` attribute to the validation rules of our `Customer` Model:

```
[Required, UniqueCustomerId]
public string ID { get; set; }
```

Filter injection

Filters are implementations of the IActionFilter, IResultFilter, IExceptionFilter, or IAuthorizationFilter interfaces that make it possible to perform special operations while invoking an action method. ASP.NET MVC allows us to apply filters in two ways, both of which are supported by Ninject:

- Applying a filter attribute to the Controller or an Action method. This approach has been supported by MVC framework since its first version and doesn't fully support DI.

- Applying filters without attributes using filter providers which is introduced in MVC 3 and supports all DI patterns.

In the first method, the filter class derives from ActionFilterAttribute and the created filter attribute will be applied to a Controller or one of its action methods. Like other attributes, a filter attribute cannot be applied if it does not have a default constructor, so we cannot use Constructor Injection in filter attributes. However, if we use Property Injection using the [Inject] attribute, the dependencies get injected by Ninject without any special configuration. The following example shows how to define an action filter attribute which can pass action information to a performance monitoring service:

```
public class PerformanceFilterAttribute : ActionFilterAttribute
{
    [Inject]
    public IPerformanceMonitoringService PerformanceMonitor
    { get; set; }

    public void OnActionExecuting(ActionExecutingContext
filterContext)
    {
        PerformanceMonitor.BeginMonitor(filterContext);
    }

    public void OnActionExecuted(ActionExecutedContext filterContext)
    {
        PerformanceMonitor.EndMonitor(filterContext);
    }
}
```

The implementation of IPerformanceMonitoringService will be injected by Ninject into the property PerformanceMonitor.

MVC3 or later versions of MVC, however, support a new way of applying filters which is DI compatible and allows all DI patterns including Construction Injection. Thus, the previous approach is not recommended in MVC3+.

The following example demonstrates how to define and apply `LogFilter` to our actions, which can log some tracking information about the called or being called action methods. The filter uses the `ILog` interface of the `Log4Net` library as a dependency:

```
public class LogFilter : IActionFilter
{
    private readonly ILog log;
    private readonly Level logLevel;

    public LogFilter(ILog log, string logLevel)
    {
        this.log = log;
        this.logLevel = log.Logger.Repository.LevelMap[logLevel];
    }

    public void OnActionExecuting(ActionExecutingContext
filterContext)
    {
        var message = string.Format(
CultureInfo.InvariantCulture,"Executing action {0}.{1}",
filterContext.ActionDescriptor.ControllerDescriptor.ControllerName,
filterContext.ActionDescriptor.ActionName);
        this.log.Logger.Log(typeof(LogFilter), this.logLevel, message,
null);    }

    public void OnActionExecuted(ActionExecutedContext filterContext)
    {
        var message = string.Format(
  CultureInfo.InvariantCulture, "Executed action {0}.{1}",
filterContext.ActionDescriptor.ControllerDescriptor.ControllerName,
filterContext.ActionDescriptor.ActionName);
 this.log.Logger.Log(typeof(LogFilter),
 this.logLevel, message, null);
    }
}
```

The LogFilter class uses the provided filterContext argument to determine the name of the Action method and its enclosing Controller. It then uses the injected implementation of ILog to log the tracking information. This class introduces two dependencies, one of which is the ILog interface and the other one is the log level under which the messages should be logged.

In order to tell MVC to use Ninject to resolve a filter, we need to register the filter using the BindFilter<TFilter> method of Kernel:

```
Kernel.BindFilter<LogFilter>(FilterScope.Action, 0)
    .WithConstructorArgument("logLevel", ("Info"));
```

The first parameter defines the filter scope whose type is System.Web.Mvc. FilterScope and the second one is a number defining the order of the filter. This information is required by MVC to instantiate and apply filters. Ninject collects this information and asks MVC on our behalf to create an instance of the given filter type and apply it to the given scope. In the previous example, LogFilter will be resolved using Ninject with "Info" as an argument for the logLevel parameter, and will be applied to all of the Action methods.

The ILog log parameter will be resolved based on how we register ILog. If you have used Log4Net before, you will remember that it can associate each logger to the type of class for which the logger is used:

```
public class MyClass
{
    private static readonly ILog log =
                        LogManager.GetLogger(typeof(MyApp));
}
```

This way, the logs can later be filtered based on their associated types.

In order to provide the required type for our logger, we bind it to a method rather than a concrete service. This way, we can use the context object to determine the type of object requiring the log:

```
Bind<ILog>().ToMethod(GetLogger);
```

The following is the code for the GetLogger method:

```
private static ILog GetLogger(IContext ctx)
{
    var filterContext = ctx.Request.ParentRequest.Parameters
                .OfType<FilterContextParameter>()
                .SingleOrDefault();
    return LogManager.GetLogger(filterContext == null ?
        ctx.Request.Target.Member.DeclaringType :
```

```
        filterContext.ActionDescriptor.ControllerDescriptor.
ControllerType);
}
```

In the previous code, the `context.Request` is the request for resolving `ILog` and `ParentRequest` is the request for resolving `LogFilter`. When a filter class is registered using `BindFilter`, Ninject provides the request with a parameter of type `FilterContextParameter`, which contains information about the context of the object to which the filter is being applied, and we can then obtain the type of the Controller class from it. Otherwise, this parameter is not provided, which means the logger is not requested by a filter class, in which case we just use the type of the class requiring the logger.

Conditional filtering (When)

Now what if we are not going to apply the filter to all of the Controllers or the action methods? Ninject provides three groups of the `WhenXXX` methods to determine in which conditions to apply the filter:

- **WhenControllerType**: This method applies the filter to the specified Controller types only.

- **WhenControllerHas**: This method applies the filter to those Controllers with the specified attribute type

- **WhenActionMethodHas**: This method applies the filter to those `Action` methods with the specified attribute type

Apart from the mentioned three groups, Ninject offers a generic `When` method, which can be used to define any custom conditions which cannot be applied using the previous methods.

The following code shows how to apply `LogFilter` to those `action` methods which have `LogAttribute`, given that the `LogAttribute` class is a simple class deriving from the `Attribute` class:

```
Kernel.BindFilter<LogFilter>(FilterScope.Action, 0)
  .WhenActionMethodHas<LogAttribute>()
  .WithConstructorArgument("logLevel", ("Info"));
```

This is another example that shows how to apply this filter to all of the actions of the `HomeController` class:

```
Kernel.BindFilter<LogFilter>(FilterScope.Controller, 0)
  .WhenControllerType <HomeController>()
  .WithConstructorArgument("logLevel", ("Info"));
```

Contextual arguments (With)

In the previous examples, we have always used a constant `"Info"` argument to be passed to the `logLevel` parameter. Apart from the standard `WithXXX` helpers, which can be used on normal bindings, Ninject provides the following `WithXXX` methods especially for filter binding:

- `WithConstructorArgumentFromActionAttribute`: It allows to get the constructor argument from the attribute which is applied to the `action` method

- `WithConstructorArgumentFromControllerAttribute`: It allows to get the constructor argument from the attribute which is applied to the Controller class

- `WithPropertyValueFromActionAttribute`: In case of Property Injection, it allows to set the property using a value from the attribute which is applied to the action method

- `WithPropertyValueFromControllerAttribute`: In case of Property Injection, it allows to set the property using a value from the attribute which is applied to the Controller class

In the following code, we get the log level from the `LogAttribute` class rather than always passing a constant string to the `logLevel` parameter:

```
Kernel.BindFilter<LogFilter>(FilterScope.Action, 0)
    .WhenActionMethodHas<LogAttribute>()
    .WithConstructorArgumentFromActionAttribute<LogAttribute>(
        "logLevel",
        attribute => attribute.LogLevel);
```

The previous code requires the `LogAttribute` class to have the `LogLevel` property:

```
public class LogAttribute : Attribute
{
    public string LogLevel { get; set; }
}
```

WCF applications

In this section, we will implement the Northwind customers scenario using **Windows Communication Foundation (WCF)**. WCF is a highly customizable and extensible framework, and it is possible to configure it to use Ninject service host factories to enable hosting of injectable services. Ninject WCF extensions include all the necessary components.

Now, add a new WCF service application to the Northwind solution, and reference `Northwind.Core` project. We also need to add reference to the `Ninject.Extensions.WCF`, `Ninject.Web.Common`, and `Ninject` libraries. We can do it either via NuGet, or we can download the binaries from the Ninject page on `GitHub`. Adding binary references manually requires some manipulations of the `Global.asax` file in our application. We talked about this approach in the last section. However, adding a reference to `Ninject.Extensions.WCF` via NuGet will also add other references to the required Ninject packages, and will create the `NinjectWebCommon` class in the `App_Start` directory of the project. Although we can use either approach, since we have used the first method in previous section, we are going to demonstrate the latter in this section. The following is the content of the `NinjectWebCommon` class:

```
public static class NinjectWebCommon
{
    private static readonly Bootstrapper bootstrapper = new
Bootstrapper();
    public static void Start()
    {
        DynamicModuleUtility
            .RegisterModule(typeof(OnePerRequestHttpModule));
        DynamicModuleUtility.RegisterModule(typeof(NinjectHttpModu
le));
        bootstrapper.Initialize(CreateKernel);
    }

    public static void Stop()
    {
        bootstrapper.ShutDown();
    }

    private static IKernel CreateKernel()
    {
        var kernel = new StandardKernel();
        kernel.Bind<Func<IKernel>>().ToMethod(ctx =>
                () => new Bootstrapper().Kernel);
        kernel.Bind<IHttpModule>()
            .To<HttpApplicationInitializationHttpModule>();

        RegisterServices(kernel);
        return kernel;
    }

    private static void RegisterServices(IKernel kernel)
    {
    // Here is our Composition Root
    }
}
```

Having the `NinjectWebCommon` class in the `App_Start` directory of our application causes the application to be started from the `Start` method of this class. The `Start` method registers the `OnePerRequestHttpModule` and `NinjectHttpModule` modules which are needed for Ninject to take care of web applications, and it initializes the Ninject bootstrapper using the kernel created in the `CreateKernel` method, which in turn calls the `RegisterServices` method. This is where we can either register our service types or load our service registration module.

Let's start by creating our `CustomerService` contract. Add a new WCF `Service` class and name it `CustomerService`. Then open the `ICustomerService` interface and add the following operations:

```
[ServiceContract]
public interface ICustomerService
{
    [OperationContract]
    IEnumerable<CustomerContract> GetAllCustomers();

    [OperationContract]
    void AddCustomer(CustomerContract customer);
}
```

We need a method for getting the list of customers, and another one to add a new customer to the repository. Since the return type of `GetAllCustomers` is not primitive, we need to define a data contract as well:

```
[DataContract]
public class CustomerContract
{
    [DataMember]
    public string ID { get; set; }
    [DataMember]
    public string CompanyName { get; set; }
    [DataMember]
    public string City { get; set; }
    [DataMember]
    public string PostalCode { get; set; }
    [DataMember]
    public string Phone { get; set; }
}
```

Now, we implement the `CustomerService` class:

```
public class CustomerService : ICustomerService
{
    private readonly ICustomerRepository repository;
```

```
    private readonly IMapper mapper;

    public CustomerService(ICustomerRepository repository, IMapper
mapper)
    {
        this.repository = repository;
        this.mapper = mapper;
    }

    public IEnumerable<CustomerContract> GetAllCustomers()
    {
        var customers = repository.GetAll();
        return mapper.Map(customers);
    }

    public void AddCustomer(CustomerContract customer)
    {
        repository.Add(mapper.Map(customer));
    }
}
```

Apart from ICustomerRepository, which is the first dependency, it needs a mapper class to map the *domain* Customer to the *contract* Customer:

```
public interface IMapper
{
    Core.Customer Map(CustomerContract customer);
    CustomerContract Map(Core.Customer customer);
    IEnumerable<CustomerContract> Map(IEnumerable<Core.Customer>
customers);
}
```

The CustomerService class has two dependencies, which are introduced in its constructor. But in order for WCF to instantiate such services which lack the default constructor, we should tell it to use Ninject's service host factories rather than the standard ones. To do so, right-click the CustomerService.svc file, and from the pop-up menu, select **View Markup**. In the markup editor of the service, add Ninject.Extensions.Wcf.NinjectServiceHostFactory as the factory of the corresponding ServiceHost:

```
<%@ ServiceHost Language="C#" Debug="true"
    CodeBehind="CustomerService.svc.cs"
    Service="Northwind.Wcf.CustomerService"
    Factory="Ninject.Extensions.Wcf.NinjectServiceHostFactory"%>
```

The `Factory` attribute can have the following values:

- `Ninject.Extensions.Wcf.NinjectServiceHostFactory` for ordinary services

- `Ninject.Extensions.Wcf.NinjectDataServiceHostFactory` for data services

Now reference the Ninject `Conventions` extension, and enter the following binding convention in the `RegisterServices` method of the `NinjectWebCommon` class:

```
kernel.Bind(x => x.FromAssembliesMatching("Northwind.*")
                  .SelectAllClasses()
                  .BindAllInterfaces());
```

ASP.NET Web Forms applications

ASP.NET Web Forms is not as extensible as MVC or WCF, and it is not possible to tweak its UI engine to support activation of pages without a default constructor. This limitation of Web Forms applications prevents making use of the Constructor Injection pattern. However, it is still possible to use other DI patterns such as an initializer method.

In order to set up Ninject for a Web Forms application, we need to add a reference to the `Ninject.Web` extension. This extension requires to have referenced `Ninject.Web.Common` and `Ninject` as well. If we use NuGet package manager, these libraries will be referenced automatically as soon as we make a reference to `Ninject.Web`. It will also create two classes in the `App_Start` directory of the application. The `NinjectWebCommon` class, which we have already discussed, and `NinjectWeb`. These classes are required by the `Ninject.Web` extension to work properly. We can add our service registrations to the `RegisterServices` method of the `NinjectWebCommon` class.

In this example, we will create a Web Form which presents a list of Northwind customers using an initializer method. Add a new ASP.NET Web Forms application to the Northwind solution, and after referencing the `Northwind.Core` project, set up Ninject as described previously.

Add a `GridView` control to the `Default.aspx` page and modify the source code of the page, as shown in the following code:

```
public partial class Default : System.Web.UI.Page
{
    private ICustomerRepository repository;

    [Inject]
```

```
    public void Setup(ICustomerRepository customerRepository)
    {
        this.repository = customerRepository;
    }

    protected void Page_Load(object sender, EventArgs e)
    {
        customersGridView.DataSource = repository.GetAll();
        customersGridView.DataBind();
    }
}
```

The `ICustomerRepository` interface is introduced as a parameter in the `Setup` method rather than a constructor parameter. That is because ASP.NET Web Forms UI engine is not configurable in such a way to instantiate UI components which don't have a default constructor. The `Setup` method will be called as soon as the `Page` object is created, having its parameter resolved and injected.

Now, reference Ninject conventions extension and put the following binding convention in the `RegisterServices` method of the `NinjectWebCommon` class:

```
kernel.Bind(x => x.FromAssembliesMatching("Northwind.*")
                 .SelectAllClasses()
                 .BindAllInterfaces());
```

Summary

Windows Forms application supports all DI patterns, because it offers a single startup location in the `Main` method and gives us the freedom of instantiating all classes ourselves. WPF and Silverlight applications are friendly to MVVM pattern, and they support all DI patterns as well. ASP.NET MVC is a DI-friendly framework, and although the creation of framework components (for example, Controllers) are up to the framework factories, it allows to replace them with Ninject factories which support injectable components. `Ninject.Web.MVC` extension contains ASP.NET MVC injection facilities of Ninject. WCF is the other web platform which supports all DI patterns because of its high extensibility and configurability. It can be configured to use Ninject service host factories which are implemented in the `Ninject.Extensions.WCF` library.

ASP.NET Web Forms does not fully support DI; however, it is possible to configure it in such a way to use some DI patterns. The `Ninject.Web` extension contains the necessary components to make use of the partial DI support to ASP.NET.

Doing More with Extensions

5

While the core library of Ninject is kept clean and simple, Ninject is a highly extensible DI container and it is possible to extend its power using extension plugins. We have already used some of them in the previous chapter. In this chapter, we will see how interception is a solution for cross-cutting concerns and how to use Mocking Kernel as a test asset. We will also look at how Ninject can be extended:

- Interception
- Mocking Kernel
- Extending Ninject

By the end of this chapter, the user will be able to make use of Interception and Mocking Kernel extensions.

Interception

There are cases where we need to do some operations before or after calling a single method or a number of methods. For example, we may need to log something before and after invoking all the methods in a component. Interception allows us to wrap the injecting dependency in a proxy object which can perform such operations before, after, around or instead of each method invocation. This proxy object can then be injected instead of the wrapped service. Ninject Interception extension creates such proxy wrappers on the fly, and allows us to intercept invocations of the wrapped service members. The following diagram shows how a service will be replaced with an intercepted one during the interception process.

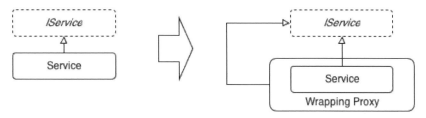

Interception is one of the best practices for implementing **Cross Cutting Concerns** such as logging, caching, exception handling, or transaction processing.

Setup Interception

Ninject Interception extension generates proxy instances based on the DynamicProxy implemented by LinFu or Castle. We can choose which implementation to use when referencing interception extension. Using NuGet either install `Ninject.Extensions.Interception.DynamicProxy` or `Ninject.Extensions.Interception.Linfu`. NuGet will also automatically install `Ninject`, `Ninject.Extensions.Interception` and `Castle.Core` or `LinFu.DynamicProxy` depending on the selected DynamicProxy implementation. In this section, we will use Castle DynamicProxy. We can also download and reference the binary files of these libraries manually. Finally, we need to add the following `using` statements to the code:

```
using Ninject.Extensions.Interception;
using Ninject.Extensions.Interception.Infrastructure.Language;
```

Member Interception

Once we have setup our project for Interception extension, some extension methods will be available via the kernel which can be used for interception. We can use these methods to intercept a method or property. Here are a few of them:

```
InterceptReplace<T> (Expression<Action<T>>, Action<IInvocation>)
InterceptAround<T> (Expression<Action<T>>,
                         Action<IInvocation>, Action<IInvocation>)
InterceptBefore<T> (Expression<Action<T>>, Action<IInvocation>)
InterceptAfter<T> (Expression<Action<T>>, Action<IInvocation>)
```

The following example shows us how to use a method interception to log around the `GetAllCustomers()` method of the `CustomerService` class:

```
Kernel.InterceptAround<CustomerService>(
    s=>s.GetAllCustomers(),
    invocation =>logger.Info("Retrieving all customers..."),
    invocation =>logger.Debug("Customers retrieved"));
```

In the preceding example, the type parameter indicates the service we are going to intercept (that is, `CustomerService`). The first parameter is a delegate which indicates the method to intercept (for example, `GetAllCustomers`). For the `InterceptAround` method, the second and third parameters are two delegates which will be executed before and after invoking the intercepted method respectively.

The `invocation` parameter whose type is `IInvocation`, provides useful information about the method invocation context. For example, we can get or change the returned value. In the following example, we will log the number of retrieved customers using the `InterceptAfter` method:

```
Kernel.InterceptAfter<CustomerService>(s=>s.GetAllCustomers(),
    invocation =>logger.DebugFormat("{0} customers retrieved",
        (IEnumerable<Customer>) invocation.ReturnValue).Count()));
```

Since the type of `ReturnedValue` is `object`, we need to cast it to reach the `Count()` method. In the following example, we will implement caching for the `GetAll()` method of the `customers` repository:

```
Kernel.InterceptReplace<SqlCustomerRepository>(
r => r.GetAll(),
invocation =>
{
    const string cacheKey = "customers";
    if (HttpRuntime.Cache[cacheKey] == null)
    {
        invocation.Proceed();
        if (invocation.ReturnValue != null)
            HttpRuntime.Cache[cacheKey] = invocation.ReturnValue;
    }
    else
        invocation.ReturnValue = HttpRuntime.Cache[cacheKey];
});
```

In this example, we used the `InterceptReplace` method, which can totally replace the functionality of the intercepted method. We used `HttpRuntime.Cache` for caching the list of `Customer` objects, which the `GetAll()` method returns. If the `Cache` object is empty, we need to call `GetAll()`, which is the intercepted method and then put the returned value in the cache. In order to call the intercepted method via the interception method (`InterceptReplace`), we should call the `Proceed()` method of the invocation object. Then, we can get its returned value, which is the list of `Customer` objects from the `ReturnValue` property of the invocation. If the `Cache` object is not empty, we just need to set the `ReturnValue` property to the cached `Customer` list. In this way, the `GetAll()` method will not be called.

The important thing to keep in mind is that the type argument provided for interception methods cannot be the type of the abstracted service. It should be the concrete implementation type. That is why we have provided `SqlCustomerRepository` rather than `ICustomerRepository` as the type argument for the `InterceptReplace` method, so the following code wouldn't work:

```
Kernel.InterceptReplace<ICustomerRepository>(
r => r.GetAll(), invocation =>{   ...   });
```

That is because interception creates a proxy wrapper around the resolved object rather than creating a new implementation of the abstracted service.

You may have noticed that all of the `InterceptXxx<T>` methods require a type argument. This obliges the application to have a reference to the dependency library, which is usually not desirable. We should be able to refer to types using their names so that we can dynamically load dependency assemblies at runtime. In order to do so, we can use the `AddMethodInterceptor` method. Here is the implementation of the preceding example using the `AddMethodInterceptor` method:

```
var repositoryType = Type.GetType(
"Northwind.SqlDataAccess.SqlCustomerRepository, Northwind.
SqlDataAccess");
Kernel.AddMethodInterceptor(repositoryType.GetMethod("GetAll"),
invocation => {     ...     });
```

Type Interception

Although method Interception targets a particular method or property of a given type, type Interception is more generalized and applies to a type or a group of types, and intercepts all of the methods and properties in a single point. In order to create an interceptor, we need to implement the `IInterceptor` interface. This interface has only one method, which is as follows:

```
void Intercept( IInvocation invocation );
```

In the following example, we will implement an exception handling interceptor which can catch the exceptions and hand them over to an exception handler service. It is the same as putting `try-catch` in all of the methods of the intercepted type:

```
public class ExceptionInterceptor : IInterceptor
{
    private IExceptionHandlerService exceptionHandlerService;
    public ExceptionInterceptor(IExceptionHandlerService
handlerService)
    {
        this.exceptionHandlerService = handlerService;
    }

    public void Intercept(IInvocation invocation)
    {
        try
        {
```

```
        invocation.Proceed();
    }
    catch (Exception exception)
    {
        exceptionHandlerService.HandleException(exception);
    }
  }
}
```

The following code shows how to add the `ExceptionInterceptor` to our convention so that it applies to all the classes of our application:

```
Kernel.Bind(x => x.FromAssembliesMatching("Northwind.*")
                    .SelectAllClasses()
                    .BindAllInterfaces()
                    .Configure(b =>
                        b.Intercept()
                            .With<ExceptionInterceptor>()
                    ));
```

The `Intercept()` method is added to the configuration section of our convention and accepts the type of the desired interceptor as its type parameter. It can then activate the provided type to create and apply the interceptor object.

If we need to intercept only a certain type in a convention rule, we can use the `ConfigureFor<T>` method:

```
Kernel.Bind(x => x.FromAssembliesMatching("Northwind.*")
                    .SelectAllClasses()
                    .BindAllInterfaces()
                    .ConfigureFor<CustomerRepository>
            (b => b.Intercept()
                            .With<ExceptionInterceptor>()
                    ));
```

If we already have an instance of our interceptor, we can use the following syntax:

```
var exceptionInterceptor = Kernel.Get<ExceptionInterceptor>();
Kernel.Bind(x => x.FromAssembliesMatching("Northwind.*")
                    .SelectAllClasses()
                    .BindAllInterfaces()
                    .Configure(b =>
                        b.Intercept()
                            .With(exceptionInterceptor)
                    ));
```

The preceding example showed how to intercept types projected by a convention. It is also possible to intercept the kernel itself. The following example applies `ExceptionInterceptor` to all of the services resolved by the kernel, no matter how they are registered:

```
kernel.Intercept(context => true)
    .With<ExceptionInterceptor>();
```

The `Intercept` method accepts a predicate, which is given an instance of the current activation context (`IContext`). This predicate indicates what services to choose for interception. In this example, we always return `true`, which means we intend to intercept all services. We can define any contextual condition by this predicate based on the activation context. Refer to the *Contextual binding* section in *Chapter3, Meeting Real-world Requirements* for refreshing how to define contextual conditions.

There is also a built-in interceptor class named `ActionInterceptor`, which can be used as a generic interceptor in case our interception logic is as simple as a single method:

```
Kernel
.Intercept()
.With(new ActionInterceptor(invocation =>
        log.Debug(invocation.Request.Method.Name)));
```

The `Interception` extension also contains an abstract `SimpleInterceptor` class, which can be extended to create interceptors with a pre/post interception logic, and an `AutoNotifyPropertyChangedInterceptor` class, which is designed specifically for WPF ViewModels and automates notification of property changes.

Multiple Interceptors

We already studied how to implement exception handling concern using interception. But what if we need to add more interceptors to a type? In reallife scenarios we usually have to implement a variety of cross-cutting concerns on each type. Multiple interception allows us to meet this requirement. The following example shows how to address both logging and exception-handling concerns using two interceptors:

```
kernel.Intercept(context => true).With<ExceptionInterceptor>();
kernel.Intercept(context => true).With<LoggerInterceptor>();
```

Alternatively, we can apply them to a convention similar to this:

```
Kernel.Bind(x => x.FromAssembliesMatching("Northwind.*")
            .SelectAllClasses()
            .BindAllInterfaces()
            .Configure(b =>
                            {
                                b.Intercept()
                                 .With<ExceptionInterceptor>();

                                b.Intercept()
                                 .With<LoggerInterceptor>();
                            }
            ));
```

We can also register multiple interceptors on a single Binding in the same way as follows:

```
var binding = Bind<IService>().To<MyService>();
binding.Intercept().With<ExceptionInterceptor>();
binding.Intercept().With<LoggerInterceptor>();
```

When we register an interceptor for a service type, Ninject no longer resolves the service by activating the service itself. Instead, Ninject returns a proxy object which wraps an instance of the service. When we call a method on the resolved object, we are actually calling the proxy implementation of that method, rather than the actual service method. The following diagram demonstrates that the proxy method invokes the `Intercept` method on the first registered interceptor:

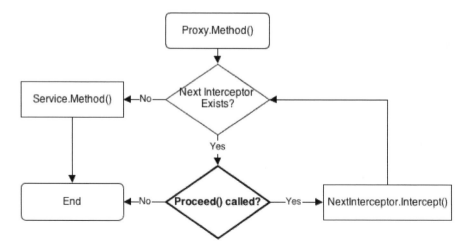

If the `Proceed` method is called within the `Intercept` method, the proxy class advances to the next interceptor and executes its `Intercept` method. Calling the `Proceed` method in the last interceptor leads to calling the actual service method. Once the actual service method is called, the control returns to the last `Intercept` method along with the value returned by the service method. Here is where the interceptor can perform post-invocation operations (for example, modifying the returned value). The control then returns to the previous interceptors one by one, until it reaches the proxy method which was initially called. The following diagram shows this sequence:

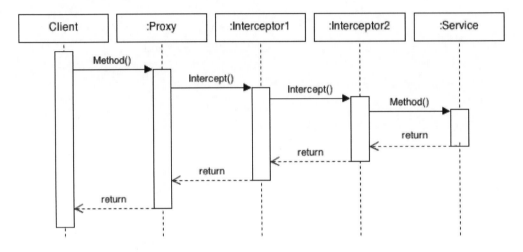

When we register multiple interceptors, the order in which they intercept can be indicated using the `InOrder` method as follows:

```
Kernel.Bind(x => x.FromAssembliesMatching("Northwind.*")
            .SelectAllClasses()
            .BindAllInterfaces()
            .Configure(b =>
                    {
                        b.Intercept()
                        .With<ExceptionInterceptor>()
                        .InOrder(1);

                        b.Intercept()
                        .With<LoggerInterceptor>()
                        .InOrder(2);
                    }
            ));
```

The lower the value of the order, the earlier the interceptor executes. So, in the preceding example, ExceptionInterceptor executes before LoggerInterceptor.

Intercept Attribute

Another way of registering an interceptor for a type or method is by using attributes. In order to create an attribute interceptor, we just need to derive from the InterceptAttribute class and override its CreateInterceptor method. In the following example, we create an attribute named InterceptExceptionsAttribute for intercepting exceptions:

```
public class InterceptExceptionsAttribute : InterceptAttribute
{
    public override IInterceptor CreateInterceptor(IProxyRequest
request)
    {
        return request.Kernel.Get<ExceptionInterceptor>();
    }
}
```

We can then apply this attribute to a method or a type as follows:

```
[InterceptExceptions]
public class Sample
{    ...    }
```

We can also apply both attributes to the same type as shown in the following code:

```
[InterceptExceptions, Log]
public class Sample
{    ...    }
```

We can apply the interceptor attributes also to methods (remember that in either way, the method should be virtual or it will not be intercepted) as follows:

```
[InterceptExceptions]
public class Sample
{
    [Log]
    public virtual void DoSomething()
    {    ...    }
    ...
}
```

In the preceding example, all of the `virtual` methods within the `Sample` class will be intercepted by `ExceptionInterceptor`. The `DoSomething` method is also intercepted by `LoggerInterceptor`.

We can also specify the order of interceptors, by setting the `Order` property of the applied attribute as follows:

```
[InterceptExceptions(Order = 2)]
public class Sample
{
    [Log(Order = 1)]
    public virtual void DoSomething()
    {    ...    }
}
```

In the preceding example, the `DoSomething` method will be intercepted first by `LoggerInterceptor` and then by `ExceptionInterceptor`.

In case if we have methods which we don't want to be intercepted, we can exclude them using the `[DoNotIntercept]` attribute as follows:

```
[InterceptExceptions]
public class Sample
{
    [Log]
    public virtual void DoSomething()
    {    ...    }

    [DoNotIntercept]
    public virtual void DoSomethingElse()
    {    ...    }
}
```

In the preceding example, although the `[InterceptExceptions]` attribute is applied to the type, it doesn't intercept the `DoSomethingElse` method.

Mocking Kernel

One of the advantages of Dependency Injection is that it improves the testability of code units and makes it even easier. Ninject has introduced Mocking Kernel, which facilitates the injection of mock objects. In this section, we will add a Test project to the `Northwind` solution and see how to use Mocking Kernel in order to write our unit tests. It is possible to extend Mocking Kernels for different isolation frameworks, and for some of them including RhinoMocks, Moq and NSubstitute, mocking kernel extensions already exist. In this example, we will use the Moq Mocking Kernel in combination with the NUnit framework to write some unit tests for the `Northwind`. `Wpf` project.

Add a new class library project named `Northwind.Wpf.Test` to the `Northwind` solution and reference the `Northwind.Wpf` and `Northwind.Model` projects. Since we are going to use some WPF components in our tests, we also need a reference to `PresentationCore`. Now using NuGet install `Ninject.MockingKernel.Moq`. It will automatically reference `Ninject`, `Ninject.MockingKernel`, and `Moq` as its prerequisites. It is also possible to download and reference binaries manually. You can use other test frameworks or Mocking Kernels according to your needs. Although there might be some slight changes, the overall process would be the same.

Now we add a new class for testing `MainViewModel` and create it as follows:

```
[TestFixture]
class MainViewModelTests
{
    private readonly MoqMockingKernel kernel;
    public MainViewModelTests()
    {
        this.kernel = new MoqMockingKernel();
    }

    [TearDown]
    public void TearDown()
    {
        kernel.Reset();
    }
}
```

The `Reset()` method clears Ninject cache of all created instances. By calling this method as part of NUnit teardown process which happens after each test, we don't need to dispose and reinitialize kernel for each test. Note that instead of `StandardKernel` we are using `MoqMockingKernel`. If there are no matching bindings for a service type, and if the type is not self-bindable, `MockingKernel` will create mock for the type and inject the associated mocked object wherever the type is requested. Thus, calling the `Get<T>()` method on `MockingKernel` will return the associated mocked object. In order to get the mock itself, the `MockingKernel` has another method named `GetMock<T>()`. We can also use the following syntax in order to explicitly define a mock binding:

```
Bind<IService>().ToMock();
```

It is useful when further setup on a binding is required:

```
Bind<IService>().ToMock()
    .WithConstructorArgument("paramName",argument)
    .InSingletonScope().Named("BindingName");
```

Let's write our first test which verifies whether getting the Customers property calls the GetAll() method of ICustomerRepository (you can review *Chapter 4, Ninject in Action* to refresh your memory if you don't remember CustomerViewModel clearly) as follows:

```
[Test]
public void GettingCustomersCallsRepositoryGetAll()
{
    var repositoryMock = kernel.GetMock<ICustomerRepository>();
    repositoryMock.Setup(r => r.GetAll());
    var sut = kernel.Get<MainViewModel>();
    var customers = sut.Customers;
    repositoryMock.VerifyAll();
}
```

In this test, calling GetMock<ICustomerRepository> returns the mock which Moq created for ICustomerRepository. We expect the GetAll() method to be called on the mocked object associated with this mock. MainViewModel is our **System under Test (SUT)** which is acquired from the kernel using the Get method. Because MainViewModel is self bindable, the kernel doesn't return a mocked object for this type and returns an instance of our own implementation of MainViewModel. Then we call the get accessor of the Customers property and verify the mock to see if the GetAll method is called on the mocked implementation of ICustomerRepository. The preceding test was a simple one and implementing it without MockingKernel wouldn't be much harder. We just needed to create mocks for other dependencies of MainViewModel and pass the associated objects to MainViewModel. In the following test we will study a more complicated case. We are going to verify whether executing CreateCustomerCommand will call the ShowDialog method of the CustomerView class:

```
[Test]
public void ExecutingCreateCustomerCommandShowsCustomerView()
{
    var customerViewMock = kernel.GetMock<ICustomerView>();
    customerViewMock.Setup(v => v.ShowDialog());
    var sut = kernel.Get<MainViewModel>();
    sut.CreateCustomerCommand.Execute(null);
    customerViewMock.VerifyAll();
}
```

Again our SUT is `MainViewModel`, but the type of mocked object is `ICustomerView`. The dependency graph of `MainViewModel` which is shown in the following diagram, shows that we need to involve other objects in this scenario in order to make the test work properly:

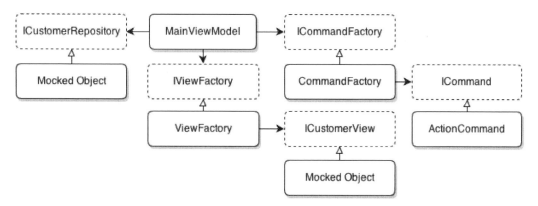

We need actual implementations of `IViewFactory`, `ICommandFactory`, and `ICommand` rather than their mocked objects. Therefore, we need the following binding rules:

```
kernel.Bind(x => x.FromAssembliesMatching("Northwind.*")
                .SelectAllClasses()
                .BindDefaultInterfaces());

kernel.Bind(x => x.FromAssembliesMatching("Northwind.*")
                .SelectAllInterfaces()
                .EndingWith("Factory")
                .BindToFactory());
```

We need to have a reference to the Ninject Factory extension (`Ninject.Extensions.Factory`) in order to create the required dynamic factories. Dynamic factory was discussed in *Chapter 3, Meeting Real-World Requirements*.

Extending Ninject

Ninject is actually a collection of single responsible components that are wired together using DI. This makes it extremely extensible, and thus new functionalities are created by adding new components and the existing behaviors can easily be customized by swapping standard components with our customized ones. All of the Ninject components are available via the `kernel.Components` property. We can also create a customized `Kernel` object by extending the `KernelBase` class or even implementing the `IKernel` interface. In order to extend `Ninject` behaviors, we need to know Ninject components and their roles. Going through all of those components is out of the scope of this book. However, we will have an example to see how to extend Ninject by adding a new component.

In the following example we will create a new `IMissingBindingResolver` component and add it to Ninject components. `IMissingBindingResolver`, as the name suggests, is responsible for resolving types for which there are no registered bindings. `SelfBindingResolver` is a preexisting example of this component which returns the type itself if it is not registered. That is why we don't need to registers types to themselves explicitly. In this example, we will create an `IMissingBindingResolver` object which can resolve any interface named `IXXX` to a type named `XXX` as follows:

```
public class DefaultImplementationBindingResolver :
     NinjectComponent, IMissingBindingResolver
{
    public IEnumerable<IBinding> Resolve (
Multimap<Type, IBinding> bindings, IRequest request)
    {
        var service = request.Service;
        if (!service.IsInterface || !service.Name.StartsWith("I"))
            return Enumerable.Empty<IBinding>();
        return new[] {
new Binding(service) { ProviderCallback = StandardProvider
.GetCreationCallback(GetDefaultImplementationType(service)) }};
    }

    private Type GetDefaultImplementationType(Type service)
    {
        var typeName = string.Format("{0}.{1}",
            service.Namespace, service.Name.TrimStart('I'));
        return Type.GetType(typeName);
    }
}
```

The `Resolve` method gets a list of bindings and the `request` object. It tries to restrict the list of bindings as much as it can and then returns the restricted list. Ideally this list should contain only one binding. We expect the service type to be an interface whose name starts with `I`. Otherwise, we return an empty list which means we cannot resolve it here. In the `GetDefaultImplementationType` method we remove `I` from the service name to achieve the name of its implementation and return its type. The type will be passed to `StandardProvider` to create a `CreationCallback` object. This callback will later be used for creating the instance. We create a new `Binding` object for this service type, having set the `CreationCallback`, and return it as a single member sequence.

The following code shows how to add this component to the kernel:

```
var kernel = new StandardKernel();
kernel.Components
.Add<IMissingBindingResolver, DefaultImplementationBindingResolver>();
```

Summary

Interception extension creates on the fly proxy wrappers around injected objects and allows us to intercept invocation of the wrapped service members and is one of the best practices to address cross-cutting concerns.

Mocking is another Ninject's handy extension which automates injection of mock objects. It has a built-in support for popular mocking frameworks such as RhinoMocks, Moq, and NSubstitute.

Ninject is a collection of independent components that are wired together and we can extend Ninject's functionality by adding new components or substituting the existing ones.

Index

A

ActionCommand 86
ActionFilterAttribute 94
Action method 96
ActivationException exception 42, 43
AddShapes method 63
antipatterns 41
ASP.NET MVC applications
    about 89-91
    filter injection 94
    validator injection 92
ASP.NET Web Forms applications 102, 103
assemblies, convention over configuration
    selecting 36
attribute-based binding 55
Attribute class 97
AutoNotifyPropertyChangedInterceptor
    class 110

B

BindAllInterfaces() 37
BindBase() 37
BindDefaultInterface() 37
BindDefaultInterfaces() 37
binding 22-24
binding, convention over configuration
    configuring 38
Binding Generator
    defining 65
Binding Resolver 54
BindingSource control 78
BindSelection(ServiceSelector selector) 38
BindSingleInterface() 37

BindToFactory method 65
BindToSelf() 38
BindUsingRegex(string pattern) 38
BindWith method 65

C

CanDecode method 48
Close method 83
CLR 17
Common Service Locator. *See* CLR
components, convention over configuration
    inclusion and exclusion, explicit 37
    selected components, filtering 37
    selecting 36
conditional filtering (When)
    about 97
    WhenActionMethodHas method 97
    WhenControllerHas method 97
    WhenControllerType method 97
ConfigurationProvider 60
ConsoleLogger class 14, 26
ConsoleLogger singleton 26
ConstraintAttribute class 52
constructor injection 42, 43
contextual arguments (With)
    about 98
    WithConstructorArgumentFromAction
        Attribute method 98
    WithConstructorArgumentFrom
        ControllerAttribute method 98
    WithPropertyValueFromActionAttribute
        method 98
    WithPropertyValueFromController
        Attribute method 98

contextual binding
  about 49-51
  attribute-based binding 55, 56
  generic helper 57
  metadata resolution 52-54
  named binding 51
  target-based conditions 56, 57
convention over configuration
  about 34, 35
  assemblies, selecting 35
  binding, configuring 38
  components, selecting 36
  service types, selecting 37, 38
Copy to Output Directory property 31
Count() method 107
CreateCustomerCommand command 116
CreateInstance method 61
CreateInterceptor method 113
CreateKernel method 89, 100
Create method
  code 80
CreateSquare method 64
CreationCallback object 119
Customer entity 75
CustomerForm
  code 79
CustomerService class
  about 101, 106
  implementing 100
CustomerViewModel class 83
CustomerWindow method 87
custom scope, object lifetime 28, 29

D

DataContext property 82
Data Transfer Object (DTO) 79
Dependency Injection. *See* DI
DI
  about 8
  containers 16
  first application 12-15
  or Inversion of Control (IoC) 9
DialogResult property 84
DI patterns 41
DoSomething method 114

dynamic factories
  about 62
  convention, using 65
  custom instance providers 68-70
  func 70
  lazy 71
  Shape Factory example 62-64
  Telecom Switch, example 66-68

E

ExceptionInterceptor interface 109
Extensible Application Markup Language
    (XAML) 81

F

Factory attribute 102
factory interface 70
factory method 61, 68
FileInfo object 47
filtering
  conditional filtering (When) 97
  contextual arguments (With) 98
filter injection 94
filters
  about 94
  applying 94
  IActionFilter 94
  IAuthorizationFilter 94
  IExceptionFilter 94
  IResultFilter 94
FromAssemblyContaining
    <SomeType>() 36
From(params Assembly[] assemblies) 36
FromThisAssembly() 36
Func 70

G

GetAllCustomers() method 106
GetAll() method 107
GetDefaultImplementationType
    method 119
GetLogger method 96
Global.asax file 90
Grab() method 11

H

HomeController class 90, 97

I

ICommand 86
IContext interface 61
ICustomerRepository 79
ICustomerRepository interface 91
ICustomerService interface 100
ICustomerValidator 93
ICustomerView 87
IInitializable interface 44
IInterceptor interface 108
IKernel interface 118
ILogger 24
ILog log parameter 96
IMissingBindingResolver component 118
IncludingNonePublicTypes() method 36
InitializeClient method 24
Initialize method 44
InjectAttribute class 93
injecting dependencies
  example 43
install-package Ninject 20
InterceptAttribute class 113
interception
  about 105, 106
  InterceptAttribute 113, 114
  member 106-108
  multiple interception 110-113
  setup 106
  types 108-110
Intercept() method 109-111
InterceptReplace method 107
InterceptXxx<T> method 108
Inversion of Control (IoC) 9
invocation parameter 107
IPerformanceMonitoringService 94
IShippersRepository 51
IsValid method 93
IView interface 87

K

KernelBase class 118
kernel.Components property 118

L

lazy object 71
LoadCustomers method 78
Load event 78
LogAttribute class 97
LogFilter class 96
logLevel parameter 96

M

MailConfig class 22
MailServerConfig object 24
MailService class 13, 15, 23
MailService type 24
Main method
  code 80
MainViewModel class 82
Mapper class
  implementing 76, 77
metadata resolution 52-54
mocking kernel 114-117
multi binding
  contextual binding 49-51
  plugin model, implementing 46-49
MvcApplication class 90
MVVM architecture
  about 81
  Model 81
  View 81
  ViewModel 81

N

named binding 51, 52
NamedLikeFactoryMethod helper
       method 68
Ninject
  about 17, 19-21
  extending 118, 119
  interception 105

official website, URL 20
official wiki, URL 17
Ninject.Extensions.Factory library 64
Ninject.Extensions.WCF library 99
NinjectHttpModule 100
Ninject library 99
Ninject modules
about 30
MailService classes, registering 30
NinjectWebCommon class 89, 99, 102
Ninject.Web.Common library 99

O

object lifetime
about 25
custom scope 28, 29
request scope 28
singleton scope 26
thread scope 27
transient scope 25
OnePerRequestHttpModule 100
OnLoad method 78
OnPropertyChanged method 84
OnStartup method 88

P

PerformanceMonitor property 94
plugin model
implementing 46-49
Proceed method 112
Proceed() method 107
providers
about 57-61
activation context 61
factory method 61, 62
Provider<T> class 58

R

RegisterServices method 100, 102
request object 119
request scope, object lifetime 28
Reset() method 115
ReturnValue property 107

S

SalutationService 21
SaveCommand property 85
Save method 85
SelectAllAbstractClasses() method 65
SelectAllIncludingAbstractClasses()
method 65
SelectAllInterfaces() method 65
SelectAllTypes() method 65
SelfBindingResolver 118
Separation of Concerns. *See* SoC
service locator 45
Service Registration 24
service types
selecting 65
service types, convention over configuration
selecting 37
ShapeService class 63
ShippersService class 50, 51
ShippersSqlRepository class 58
ShowDialog method 84
Silverlight applications
about 81
using 81-88
SimpleInterceptor class 110
singleton scope, object lifetime 26
SoC 10
SqlCustomerRepository 38
StandardInstanceProvider 68
StandardProvider 57
Start() method 89
SwitchService class 67
System Under Test (SUT) 12, 116

T

target-based conditions 56
Target object 60
TextBox controls 78
thread scope, object lifetime 27
transient scope, object lifetime 25

U

Unblock button 20
UniqueCustomerIdAttribute class 93
User.Current 29

V

validator injection 92, 93

W

WCF 98
WCF applications 98
WhenInjectedInto<T> method 57
Windows Forms 77
Windows Presentation Foundation.
       See WPF applications
WPF applications
  about 81
  using 81-88

X

XML configuration
  about 31
  using 31-34

Thank you for buying
Mastering Ninject for Dependency Injection

About Packt Publishing

Packt, pronounced 'packed', published its first book "*Mastering phpMyAdmin for Effective MySQL Management*" in April 2004 and subsequently continued to specialize in publishing highly focused books on specific technologies and solutions.

Our books and publications share the experiences of your fellow IT professionals in adapting and customizing today's systems, applications, and frameworks. Our solution based books give you the knowledge and power to customize the software and technologies you're using to get the job done. Packt books are more specific and less general than the IT books you have seen in the past. Our unique business model allows us to bring you more focused information, giving you more of what you need to know, and less of what you don't.

Packt is a modern, yet unique publishing company, which focuses on producing quality, cutting-edge books for communities of developers, administrators, and newbies alike. For more information, please visit our website: www.packtpub.com.

About Packt Open Source

In 2010, Packt launched two new brands, Packt Open Source and Packt Enterprise, in order to continue its focus on specialization. This book is part of the Packt Open Source brand, home to books published on software built around Open Source licences, and offering information to anybody from advanced developers to budding web designers. The Open Source brand also runs Packt's Open Source Royalty Scheme, by which Packt gives a royalty to each Open Source project about whose software a book is sold.

Writing for Packt

We welcome all inquiries from people who are interested in authoring. Book proposals should be sent to author@packtpub.com. If your book idea is still at an early stage and you would like to discuss it first before writing a formal book proposal, contact us; one of our commissioning editors will get in touch with you.

We're not just looking for published authors; if you have strong technical skills but no writing experience, our experienced editors can help you develop a writing career, or simply get some additional reward for your expertise.

Refactoring with Microsoft Visual Studio 2010

ISBN: 978-1-849680-10-3   Paperback: 372 pages

Evolve your software system to support new and ever-changing requirements by uploading your C# code base with patterns and principles

1. Make your code base maintainable with refactoring

2. Support new features more easily by making your system adaptable

3. Enhance your system with an improved object-oriented design and increased encapsulation and componentization

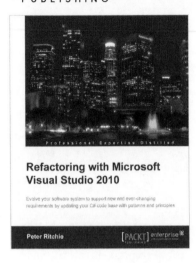

JBoss Weld CDI for Java Platform

ISBN: 978-1782160-18-2   Paperback: 122 pages

Learn CDI concepts and develop modern web applications using JBoss Weld

1. Learn about dependency injection with CDI

2. Install JBoss Weld in your favorite container

3. Develop your own extension to CDI

4. Decouple code with CDI events

5. Communicate between CDI beans and AngularJS

Please check **www.PacktPub.com** for information on our titles

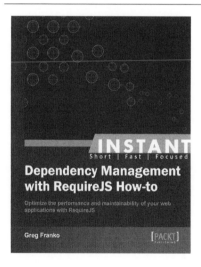